A significant report... Armed with the writings of Ernest Becker and Carl Jung, Vic Van Valin invites us on a psychological foray through the preening consumerism and group think of modern living in his search for a more meaningful life, a search which, to his surprise and despite his admitted failings, leads to a religious attitude of love and concern for others. I heartily commend this book to you.

Daniel Liechty, Assoc. Professor of Social Work
Illinois State University, Normal, IL

This fine book starts with Ernest Becker's "denial of death" and lets us tag along on the author's personal pilgrimage from such denial through a metaphoric reading of scripture to a faith in the power of love to make us "count" in the cosmic scheme.

Neil Elgee, founder and president
The Becker Foundation, Seattle, WA

CASTING OUT FEAR

VICTOR VAN VALIN

Outskirts Press, Inc.
Denver, Colorado

v7.0 r1.0

Outskirts Press, Inc.
http://www.outskirtspress.com

ISBN: 978-1-4327-0996-9

PRINTED IN THE UNITED STATES OF AMERICA

PREFACE

Me, you, all of us arrive in this world with no clue as to what we are supposed to do with our lives. Yet every moment of every day we are faced with questions that call for the making of choices: How should I respond to and deal with this opportunity? Or that setback? What should I do about a troubled relationship? Why did I react the way I did to what someone else did or said? How should I have reacted? Should I be focusing my efforts on this goal or that goal? Since I will die someday, is pursuing any goal a pointless exercise? Who cares? Does how I conduct my life in the here and now have any bearing on coming to terms with the gruesome fact of my inevitable death?

Before falling asleep at night I would lie in bed mulling over the choices presented by such questions.

And this is the book I wish I had had on my nightstand to help me make the right choices---

because my life (and yours) amounts to the sum of such choices.

Understanding why we make the choices that we do---why we behave the way we do---requires becoming aware of the mostly hidden fears, desires and biases that motivate us and drive our choices. Thus, in my 30s I began a study of human psychology. In the course of this study I was introduced to the writings of Ernest Becker (1924-1974) through his book *The Denial of Death*, for which he posthumously won the 1974 Pulitzer Prize for non-fiction. Becker was trained as a cultural anthropologist and was an academic, not a practicing psychoanalyst. But in *The Denial of Death* and his other writings he synthesized into one general theory of human behavior the theories of Sigmund Freud, Otto Rank and others. I also read widely of the writings of Carl G. Jung (1875-1961). Becker's and Jung's theories of human behavior have become my lodestar in matters of psychology.

But as valuable as an understanding of human psychology may be in helping us discern why we made the choices we made in the past, modern social/psychoanalytical science has not as yet come up with a consensus prescription for what new direction our lives may need to take to attain a sense of positive well-being and contentment. Each of us is seemingly left to find our own way out of the mess that makes up our life.

You will find a strong vein of religion running through this book. First, I would question the correctness of any purportedly scientific explanation of the human condition and why we behave the way we do unless it found some corroboration in the West's most influential and widely read literary work—the Bible. At a minimum, it is a masterwork of psychological insights into human behavior. Secondly, many in the social/psychoanalytical field, most notably Freud, were atheists and viewed the religious beliefs of the Judeo-Christian tradition, at least if taken literally, as wishful thinking and a sign of child-like dependency. Becker and Jung were among the few such scientists that believed in the value, even the necessity, of developing a religious outlook (regardless of whether one subscribes to a specific religious creed or joins a church) as a condition to quelling men's fears, particularly our fear of death, and acquiring a sense of peaceful equanimity. I needed to explore what they meant by the term "religious outlook" and how one might go about developing such an outlook.

Thus, this book is about my search for answers as to what I am supposed to do with my life and how to deal with my death. I hope it may stimulate your own thinking on such matters as you work your way through your own life.

DEDICATION

This book is dedicated to my sister, Ginnie, and my wife, Liz, who taught me most of what I know and our children, Vanessa, Jonathan, Jeffrey and John, who saw to it that I learned what I had been taught.

A human being is a part of the whole, called by us the "Universe." He experiences himself, his thoughts and feelings, as something separated from the rest, a kind of optical delusion of his consciousness. This delusion is a kind of prison for us, restricting us to our personal desires and to affection for a few persons nearest to us. Our task must be to free ourselves from this prison by widening our circle of compassion to embrace all living creatures and the whole of nature…

Albert Einstein in a letter to a friend

TABLE OF CONTENTS

Chapter 1
DENIAL AND DELUSION

It is man's tragic destiny: he must desperately justify himself as an object of primary value in the universe; he must stand out, be a hero, show that he *counts.*

Ernest Becker in *The Denial of Death*

As I now look back at that time I clearly see that apart from animal instincts [what] affected my life...[was] a desire to be better not in my own eyes or in the eyes of God, but rather a desire to be better in the eyes of other people. And this effort to be better in the eyes of other people was very quickly displaced by a longing to be stronger than other people, that is, more renowned, more important, wealthier than others.

Leo Tolstoy in *Confession*

When we emerge from the dark warm cavern of our mother's womb into the blinding light and chill air, when the thick knotty cord that binds us to her is finally cut through and, in panic, we gulp down our first breath, we begin to realize that *we are a being who exists separate and apart from all other things in nature*. As we unfold, get our child's unsteady legs under us and commence stumbling and strutting across the stage of life, it is the relentless, glaring spotlight of our own consciousness of self and our self-absorbed focus on our invisible inner moods, feelings, fantasies and thoughts which keeps us separated from one another and the rest of nature. The eerie sense that we are being followed and watched from on high as we move through life is but a projection of this painful self-consciousness onto the screen of the universe.

And it is this self-conscious awareness of ourselves as separate entities combined with our miraculous capacity for rational thought, memory and imagination that so dramatically differentiates us from nature's other animals. In comparison to other creatures, the degree to which our behavior is driven by instincts is minimal. And our minds can soar! We can mentally reach out to the stars and speculate about how the universe was born. We can mathematically deduce the existence of atomic particles so microscopically tiny we do not yet have other means of confirming their actual existence. We can imagine ourselves living in a heaven or a hell or another incarnation. By contrast, nature's other creatures live out their lives mostly just following their noses, their behavior governed by the instincts encoded in their genes.

They do not question how they and the rest of nature came to be. They do not foresee their own death. They do not inquire as to the meaning of their lives or think about their place in the cosmic order.

Only humans contemplate such matters. And when we do we come to the awesome, humbling realization that we have been blessed with the gift of life and the ability to replicate ourselves, a gift that arose in the mists of the primordial past and moves like a great river through us into generations yet to come. But we are also brought to the trembling realization that, as with nature's other creatures, *our lives are ephemeral and will end with the worms.* Our soaring, ethereal, spiritual self is forever shackled to a rotting, stinking body that will eventually slough away. However hard we try, we cannot wriggle free of our animal carcass. We cannot leave it behind, like the spent casing of an emerging insect, and fly away. And even more terrifying*, our lives have no apparent cosmic significance or meaning*. In spite of our uniqueness and special gifts, any memory or other trace of our having ever lived is likely to survive our death only very briefly. And of all of nature's creatures, apparently *only we are consciously aware of such an ignominious fate.*

Yet the vast majority of people appear to be untroubled by their existential situation: their lonely set-apart-ness, their cosmic powerlessness and insignificance, their finitude. On the surface they seem to be oblivious to our perilous situation. How we might reconcile ourselves to such a fate is virtually never discussed. It is not a topic of conversation I have heard discussed at dinner parties or family events. Nor has it been the focus of any church sermons or public lectures I have attended. Most people seem to just shrug it off. But is there any subject of more crucial importance to us? Just to put such thoughts down on paper causes my hand to shake. They put a dagger to the heart of my narcissistic urge for self-preservation. *To be nothing is to be nonexistent*! If we are nothing and all is vanity, then what purpose is served, what use is there in striving to overcome the trials and tribulations of our daily lives? Doesn't the inescapable logic of the existential situation into which we are born lead us to the brink of suicide or madness?

Our silence on a matter of such crucial importance is deafening! And it tells us something. As Ernest Becker and others in the psychoanalytic field would describe it, our self-consciousness, our isolating sense of estrangement and our cosmic powerlessness and insignificance, combined with the awareness of our certain death, generate anxieties and fears of such horrific intensity that we cannot hold them in our conscious minds. So we repress them and push them down into our unconscious. To avoid the terror of openly acknowledging our set-apart-ness, our pitiable impotence and our inevitable death and to keep our lives moving forward, we deny the truth about our existential situation and refuse to face up to its reality.

To more fully understand what Becker and others are telling us, we need only to return to our childhood. As young children, we typically find ourselves simply overwhelmed by life. It clutches and claws at us, tripping us up and testing our powers at every turn. It is full of surprises and unexpected dangers—dogs that bite, bees that sting, branches that break. The nights hold spooky unknowns and dreams often turn into nightmares.

The miracle and majesty of nature is overpowering. We are confronted with vast skies, massive mountains, surf pounding oceans and towering forests. We may be witnesses to or otherwise learn about such shattering events as avalanches, volcanic eruptions, earthquakes, hurricanes and floods. Nature comes at us with a breathtaking variety of howling, growling, chirping, buzzing creatures. We easily become lost in woods that entangle us and hills and valleys which disorient us. When we look up at the night sky, we become aware that our planet is but a speck in a vastly larger universe of billions of other heavenly bodies. Faced with the abundance, power and vastness of the natural world, a child is left reeling in a state of awe and wonder, left feeling puny and helpless.

And when we compare ourselves to our parents and other adults in our lives, we are dwarfed by their size and strength and cowed by their worldly knowledge and ability to perform all manner of tasks far beyond a child's capacity to do or understand. We have neither the physical prowess nor the know-how to provide for even the most basic of our needs for food, shelter and safety. When faced by its surrounding human reality, a child is again reduced to feeling impotent, inept and worthless. And as we enter our early teens, we further begin to grasp, however vaguely, that we, along with all our hopes and dreams, will one day die and vanish into oblivion.

To keep from facing the possibility that we are nothing in the cosmic scheme of things, to keep from being brought to our knees by the terror arising from experiencing the world as it really is, we banish the existential anxieties and fears from our conscious minds. We deny our experience of the natural world by laying aside our sense of awe and wonder and simply ignoring the implications of our inevitable death. By such repression and denial, we are able to tame our terror, acquire a semblance of emotional stability and accumulate enough confidence in our own meager powers to get on with our lives. We lie to ourselves about our existential fears, impotence and mortality and the miraculousness of our own existence in order to keep our terror in check. Such denial enables us to develop and maintain a sense of self-sufficiency and independence, to move forward as if we were truly in charge of our lives and masters of our fate.

However, in the dark recesses of our psyches, our repressed existential anxieties and fears churn and ferment and give rise to compensatory desires to be admired and respected, to be more successful, wealthier, more powerful or in other ways superior to others. Our existential fears generate in us a compulsive drive to be esteemed, to have our lives validated as significant and ourselves considered valuable and important. We must feel and believe, as Becker observed in the quote at the beginning of this chapter, that we *count* in the cosmic scheme of things. And by counting in the cosmic scheme, we establish a link to that which is eternal and infinite and obtain a taste of immortality, thereby dissolving some of the fear generated by our awareness of our inevitable death!

The human child's unusually long period of helplessness results in almost complete dependence upon their parents to provide for the child's physical needs and safety, not just for a few weeks or months but for many years. Such extended dependency, says Becker, causes children to elevate their parents to the status of minor deities. It further generates in the child a tremendous desire to please their parents and thereby provide the child with some assurance of their continued support and protection. And the child soon learns what behavior earns hugs and smiles and praises from his or her parents and what behavior triggers harsh voices, frowns and other punishment. Children also learn that, by altering their own behavior, by declining to act on various impulses, they can more predictably secure parental approval and thereby avoid arousing any anxiety about their continued care and affection.

Further, having been born with only minimal instincts, as children we have no inkling as to how we are supposed to act in this world, what we are supposed to do with our lives and how we should deal with the fact of our unavoidable death. The answers to such questions not being self-evident, we look to our parents and the culture into which we are born to provide us with answers. Thus, the child becomes programmed not only to seek the approval of parents and other adults, but to look to them for guidance as to what to do in order to bring a sense of order, purpose and meaning into their life. With scarcely a critical thought, the child voluntarily, even eagerly, conforms his behavior to the patterns of thinking and the mores and modes of conduct modeled and approved by those around him. As youngsters, we do so to earn the approval of our parents. Later we do so not only to maintain the continued support of our family, but to gain the esteem of our peers in society at large.

By the time we are ready to leave home and cease being dependent on our families, we will have developed what Freud called a superego, that is, we will have unconsciously and uncritically transferred and handed over to others much of our capacity for self-governance. We will have internalized as our own the beliefs, attitudes and values sanctioned as being right and proper by the social group and culture to which we belong. Thus, when we do something that merits society's approval, we will experience a rush of self-congratulatory ego inflation, a feeling of accomplishment and well-being, *just as if* our parents had been there to personally applaud our performance. Unwittingly, we have become, in Becker's word, "reinstinctivized," that is, programmed to compulsively chase after the esteem of our peers. We have been so programmed, not by nature, but as a compensatory reaction to our existential situation and our unconscious transference to others of the power to formulate our beliefs, values and attitudes.

Denial And Delusion

The hidden flame that burns so hot within us is our unconscious yearning and intense compensatory desire to be accepted and respected, to occupy a position of power and control, to be in charge and successful. It is a desire not at the margin of our lives, but an achingly acute desire *at the very core of it.* We spend most of our waking lives compulsively trying to prove ourselves, trying to become heroes in the eyes of others. Further, if we can become heroes in the eyes of others, then we may be remembered long after our death and thereby attain a tiny measure of immortality.

Unfortunately, esteem is not something that can be generated by oneself. It must be earned. It is bestowed upon us from without, by our families and peers, by the culture in which we live and move. We get it by internalizing and adopting as our own the values, attitudes and beliefs that *they* hold to be true. We get it by offering up our unique individuality and conforming our beliefs and behavior to the ideological idols and cultural rituals and practices *they* deem to be correct and proper.

All cultures are ever-evolving, arbitrary fabrications of the human mind. A culture's worldview or belief system, the attitudes, customs and behavior generally accepted by its members as being correct and proper, will vary from one society to another and from one historical period to another. One of the principal functions of a culture's worldview is to provide its members with a hero system, a set of values, conventions and modes of conduct that, if adopted and followed, will earn them the esteem of their peers. When we buy into the hero system of our culture, we acquire a framework for our lives, an answer to the question of how we are supposed to act in this world, while simultaneously obtaining the stamp of approval from our peers that validates our lives as ones that count. Thus, we spend most of our lives performing, trying to earn the applause and respect of our families and peers. We eagerly play to one another with little awareness that we are on stage, caught up in the dramas written by our families and peers and the culture in which we live. And we do not recognize our behavior as obsessive/compulsive, even neurotic, because of being built on a foundation of fear and denial. Since nearly all of us are engaged in it, we see such behavior as perfectly *normal*!

As an illustration of how our sense of self-worth is derived from the status symbols provided by one's culture, it is, of course, no secret that in the mainstream of present-day Western society one's esteem is enhanced by wearing the latest designer clothes, driving an expensive new car, acquiring an address in a tony neighborhood and belonging to the right clubs. We seek to acquire such things not for their inherent value as clothing, transportation, shelter or a place to socialize but because of their value as symbols of our personal worth.

Not all people within a given culture will necessarily be attracted to the same status symbols. The symbols will vary from person to person, depending upon the particular niche within a culture we occupy. For instance, a doctor's sense of self-worth may be derived not only from the admiration of his patients for his professional expertise, but also from the honor of being chosen by his peers to serve on a select committee of medical professionals. An athlete may measure his self-esteem mostly by his continued ability to place high in various competitions, selection to an all-star team or by the number of trophies in his display case. A bureaucrat's self-esteem may depend on whether he has gained a corner office or a prized parking space.

But whether ironworker or artist, hippie or yuppie, mechanic or corporate mogul, each of us seeks a place in society consistent with our gifts (good looks, smarts, musical abilities, etc.) and interests from which we can extract not just a livelihood but a generous dose of esteem.

Thus, with varying degrees of conscious awareness, we constantly compare ourselves to others. It is vital to our self-esteem to be sure that we have not fallen behind the Joneses. To maintain our place on the social ladder, we look for things about others that entitle us to criticize, belittle or otherwise look down on them. Our sensitivities are finely calibrated to detect even the smallest of slights to our station or authority. In spite of all its subtle nuances, we play the game of one-upmanship like grand masters and hardly give it a thought. However much we may individually differ in how we play the game, the point is that most of us continually and obsessively engage in trying to do something that entitles us to the admiration and respect of our peers. We do so in order to maintain the pretense that we are truly *somebody* in the cosmic scheme of things, that some memory of us will survive our death and we will therefore be entitled to claim a sip from the cup of immortality.

According to Becker, the two most widely adopted styles or modes of behavior humans have devised to cover up and deny our fears of insignificance, powerlessness and death and provide the illusion that we are somebody, that we are heroes, that our lives have some cosmic value and upon our death we can expect to enjoy some small measure of immortality are the "immersion in the group" and the "sticking-out" modes of heroic behavior.

Denial And Delusion

The immersion in the group mode asks us to surrender our individual uniqueness, submerge ourselves in and take our identity from a larger religious/political/social or other group drawn from the culture in which we live. By submersion in the larger group, we erase any feeling we have of being split off, isolated and alone, and replace it with an expansive sense of connectedness to others. We become energized by drawing in the lifeblood of being welcomed, accepted and validated by the group's other members. We feel strengthened by the group's larger numbers. When a group's leaders teach that its members are somehow special or superior, they tap into our need to feel we are better and more important than others. We swell with self-righteousness and pride.

We like to think of ourselves as self-sufficient, independent and fully capable of making our own judgments and decisions. This self-image helps us cover up the reality of our existential impotence. But as Erich Fromm has so eloquently argued, just as an overwhelmed child looks to his or her parents for nurturing and guidance, we all carry into adulthood an unadmitted readiness and yearning to be taken care of, a willingness to uncritically buy into the expectations of the group. We are all too eager to blindly follow and idealize its leaders in exchange for the oceanic feeling of at-oneness generated by being absorbed into the group's larger reality. Such immersion relieves us of the daily grind of striving to take responsibility for our lives, of constantly recreating ourselves as better, more important, more successful than others. And by becoming members of a larger group, we become integrated into an ongoing, transcendent order that will carry on after our death. Thus, immersion in a larger group holds out the tantalizing possibility of providing us with a taste of immortality!

Perhaps marriage and the creation of a family is the most basic and obvious example of our denial and repression of our existential fears by immersion in a larger order for the purpose of forging a link to the eternal and the immortal. By giving birth to sons and daughters who in turn marry and produce further generations of sons and daughters we become a part of nature's eternally revolving wheel of birth and death and rebirth. Sexual desire is nature's teaser. It is an ecstatic gift designed to entice us into sexual union and survival of the species. When such union occurs solely for its own sake, for the immediate pleasure it provides, it is an act of electrically-charged lust. But when it occurs in the context of a trusting surrender of individual egos, as a reaffirmation of a couple's commitment to serve and nurture one another and a celebration of their joinder in the common enterprise of marriage and family, then two become separate parts of one whole and their union becomes an act of love and connection to the eternal generative energies of the universe.

Another widely adopted means for seeking immortality via immersion in a group has been through our religious beliefs and practices. Christianity, for example, envisages an invisible, larger reality that envelops and surrounds us. It is presided over by an intelligent energy/being called God and his host of angels and archangels. God, we are told, intervenes in human affairs by granting or withholding his beneficence, depending on how we behave. We affirm our membership in the larger order of believers by regularly attending church services in which we, in unison with our friends and neighbors, confess our errors and give thanks to Him while humbly kneeling. And those who are repentant are explicitly promised that upon their death their souls, their unique spiritual essence, will be granted a blissful, eternal afterlife in a place known as "heaven."

We also express our hidden existential fears and their compensatory desires for fame, fortune and immortality through immersion by participating in a variety of political, professional and social groups—by becoming active in some patriotic cause, in promoting a particular ethnic or racial heritage or by joining various political or professional groups. By surrendering our egos to the expectations and will of such groups, we become accepted, valued members. When the group's activities are deemed laudable (protecting the nation against its enemies, for example), being a member of the group entitles us to individually accept as our own any accolades and praise showered on the group.

When the group preaches that its members are somehow special—part of a select elite, members of a superior race, God's chosen, the vanguard of history—our sense of value and importance becomes even more inflated. Simply by joining such a group, its members become entitled to personally draw around themselves the mantle of its claims to superiority and any assertion that its values, ideology or heritage are somehow more true or better or more glorious than those of other groups. By identifying with such a group, we become bound together as defenders of the faith, soldiers in the army of the righteous, blood brothers and sisters, comrades in arms! Our lives seem favored by destiny.

And since the group will carry on after our death, our lives are also granted that which we, as individuals, cannot otherwise obtain: an afterlife and a link to the eternal. By submersion in the group, we are able to take a tiny sip from the holy grail of immortality!

The "sticking-out" mode of heroic behavior is

the second means mankind has devised to cover up and deny our fears of insignificance, impotency and death and generate a sense of cosmic value and importance and thereby reach for immortality. It is at the other end of the spectrum from passively burying our egos in the group. In sticking-out from the group we strive to express our individuality and uniqueness, to make a mark, to rise above our neighbors, to be more successful than our peers in doing what *they* deem worthy of admiration and respect. We buy a pricey new car, take an expensive vacation, press for a higher management position or seek a seat on the board of our favorite charity, not only out of need or altruism, but also to make a statement, to prove to others that we are important, that we count. And if we work hard enough, with a little luck we may attain such success as will enable us to erect monuments to ourselves: establish a corporate colossus or a charitable foundation or fund a hospital wing, all with our name writ large over the front door. Here again do we not catch the strong scent of humankind's denial of our creaturely finitude and our heroic striving for some tiny measure of immortality?

Except perhaps for the artist in search of his own unique view of the world, both the strategies of immersion in the group and sticking-out from the group require us to conform our thinking and behavior to what our culture or subculture values and approves. Thus, our lives are spent onstage with one eye self-consciously cocked on whether the audience of our families and peers is paying attention to us. And both strategies involve constructing a fictional self. They require that we delude ourselves into thinking we or the group in which we are immersed are somehow special or superior, all so we may avoid acknowledging the painful reality of our cosmic insignificance and ultimate death.

We employ these two strategies almost unconsciously, slipping seamlessly back and forth between them, as the moment permits. For a simplistic example, take a sporting event such as a football game. At the outset of the contest the spectators and players stand up and sing the national anthem, an experience that evokes a feeling of unity and at-oneness among all the people in the stadium. Then, down on the field, the players complete their final warm-ups for the contest, each hoping to out-finesse and dominate their opposite on the other team, thereby demonstrating their superiority. Each player nurtures the dream that they can somehow make a play that will lead their team to victory and make them a hero in the eyes of his teammates and fans. As the contest begins, each set of fans sends up an excited cheer for their respective team, eagerly hoping to vicariously share in the thrill of victory and bask in the glow of their team's superiority over the other team.

All of us are constantly switching from one strategy to the other and back again, but any particular individual may tend to employ one style of heroics more often than the other depending upon their gender, personal life history, cultural conditioning, character and where they are in their life cycle. A young man emerging from adolescence and seeking to gain independence from his family may lean to the sticking-out style of becoming a hero. A middle-aged man may marry a younger, trophy wife to avoid admitting to himself that he is getting older and to impress his friends. A woman may seek out a man who is ambitious and seems destined to succeed in whatever career he chooses in order that she can bask in the heightened social status his success will provide her. An older person who has weathered the career wars of his or her middle years may gravitate toward the immersion style of heroism. Similarly, those who may be a little shy and introverted and prone to avoiding confrontations may more often rely on the strategy of surrendering their egos to a group. Those who are more extroverted, competitive and ambitious may strive to elevate themselves above their peers and lean toward the sticking-out style of heroics.

The blend of strategies will also vary depending upon the ideological/cultural worldview of the society in which one lives. For example, certainly the traditional Confucian cultures of China, Korea and Japan have encouraged their people to earn the esteem of their peers by submerging themselves in the group. Just as clearly, the current ideological and cultural value system of capitalist Western society has reinforced widespread adoption of the sticking-out style of heroism. The philosopher/psychologist Sam Keen has labeled the latter cultural worldview the "Western Myth," a myth grounded in the masculine traits of aggressive action, power and control: war, competition and conflict make the world go round, not love. Survival of the fittest is the ultimate reality and unrestrained aggressiveness our true nature. Progress is measured by the extent of our material acquisitions and our ability to control and exploit nature. Working and getting ahead is our creed.

Thus, we determinedly seek a better education and skills, in part for the satisfaction inherent in doing something well, but also in the hope of proving ourselves and earning more respect and material rewards than our peers. We jockey and shove for positions of power and control in our families, workplaces and communities. We strive for superiority and success on the playing fields. We frantically reach for fame and fortune. We crave all the badges, perks and notoriety that go with being the best, with being right, in charge, wielding power and getting the most attention.

Denial And Delusion

In pulling together the various strands and synthesizing late 19th and early to mid 20th century psychoanalytical thought, Becker sought to provide a general unified-field explanation of human behavior: Why do we behave the way we do? I certainly would not presume to assess the ability of his synthesis to account for human behavior in all historical periods and across all cultures. I can, however, be a witness to whether it cogently explains my life, why I made the decisions I did and behaved the way I did in the historical moment and culture in which I was born and raised. And to the extent it rings true, I can follow up on its implications as to whether and to what degree I can cast aside my cultural programming, slip out of my public persona, take charge of my life, find my authentic self and lead a more meaningful life.

A little background on me therefore becomes necessary. I was born in the late 1930s and raised in a small town in the Pacific Northwest not far from Seattle, Washington. I grew up on World War II's patriotic war movies and Randolph Scott and John Wayne westerns. I graduated from the town's only public high school in the mid-1950s. On a whim generated by the request of business friend of my father, I had applied for admission to his alma mater, Williams College, a small, then all-male, private liberal arts college in New England. I knew nothing about the college other than what I gleaned from the materials which the admissions office had sent me. Nor had I previously given any thought about attending a school so far from my hometown. But when they offered me a partial scholarship, I accepted. I arrived on campus thinking I might become a creative writer. However, after being asked to write a short essay as a test of my writing skills, I was promptly thrown into a remedial writing class. This was not an auspicious beginning for my college career (or the writing of this book)!

During my college years I strove to be the best that I could be (not in the sense of being the best person I could be, but in the sense of being good at my occupation as a student). It was a very competitive school and I was only modestly successful as a student. A topic occasionally brought up but seldom pursued was the need for a "philosophy of failure," some rationale that would allow us middling students to feel good about ourselves. No such philosophy coming to hand, I worked quite hard at trying to get good marks.

I majored in American history and literature, a field that held few employment prospects, but, as hindsight reveals, provided an excellent primer on the mid-20th century American worldview and value system from which I sprang. (Thus, it provided a wonderful backdrop for undertaking the discovery of who I was and who I might want to become. Was choosing such major just a lucky accident? Or was something else at work to cause me to make such a choice?)

Had I been asked why I was working so hard in a major that had such poor prospects, I would have been dumbfounded by the question. It was certainly not a question I asked myself. Should not one always do their best in any endeavor they undertook? I would probably have mumbled something about getting good marks to test myself, to see how I measured up among my peers or to give me a leg up in prying open some future occupational door. I was in awe of the braininess and talents of my classmates (many of whom had fine private prep school backgrounds). However, with a little further prodding, I might have admitted that it was also important to me that my classmates have a favorable opinion of me. Gaining the approval and respect of my peers seemed like a natural, rational desire and goal.

But I would have vehemently denied any suggestion that my striving for achievement and acceptance was due to an unconscious desire to uphold the family honor and obtain my parents' approval, a deep compulsive need to prove myself vis-à-vis my peers, an obsessive, competitive impulse to stick-out, to be more successful than they were. And I would have vigorously rejected the notion that such needs and desires were driven by a trembling fear of cosmic insignificance and impotence and anxiety over my inevitable death!

Chapter 2
THE INVISIBLE KINGDOM

> As a Scot and a Presbyterian [minister], my father believed that man by nature was a mess...
>
> Norman Maclean in *A River Runs Through It*

> The evil deeds that I do not desire to do are what I am ever doing.
>
> Paul in Romans 7:19

The psychological insight of Freud and his successors that has been the most difficult for me to fully grasp and appreciate is the extent to which my behavior is driven, not by conscious, well thought-out reasons but by invisible, emotionally charged fears, desires and attitudes lying in my unconscious. According to the psychologists, we commence the difficult journey of life aware of ourselves as set apart and estranged from all other things in nature. We also undertake the journey *estranged from our inner selves*—from any awareness, as the father of Norman Maclean's hero succinctly put it, of the "mess" that makes up the invisible world of the unconscious.

Thus it follows that if we are to take charge of our lives, we must become *consciously* aware of the shadowy, emotionally-charged energies of the unconscious which cause us to behave compulsively, reflexively, often in ways, as noted by Saint Paul in the above quote, contrary to our expressly stated intentions and goals. This is not just a task for the dysfunctional and neurotic. It is also a necessary, virtually unavoidable undertaking for those of us who would like to believe that we are somewhat "normal."

In exploring this mess, Freud and his fellow psychologists started with the portion of the psyche that is conscious of oneself as a tiny fragment split off from the rest of the universe. They called it the "ego." The ego is the "I" within us, the center of conscious self-awareness and rational intellectualization. It attempts to consciously assimilate and mediate the endless stream of often conflicting input that moves in and out of our heads, accepting some materials while rejecting or repressing others. The input comes from two directions. One face of the ego is turned outward, toward the external world. The other face is turned inward, toward the inner world of the unconscious. The ego serves as the hub for all interaction between these two worlds and the filter for reconciling any conflicting input.

The ego takes the information it receives from

the external world, including the factual circumstances immediately confronting us, and attempts to integrate such input in some orderly, rational way with the demands and expectations of our families and peers and the values and attitudes they have passed on to us as well as the fears, desires, impulses and intuitions that bubble up from the inner world of the unconscious. By bringing some modicum of order to our psyche, our ego is attempting to chart a course and move forward the ship we call our life.

However, the psychologists also tell us that our ego is afloat on a large unsettled sea of unconsciousness, an ocean swarming with shadowy, shape-shifting fears, desires, attitudes and biases that may rise to the surface as fiery displays of anger, enervating depressive moods, incapacitating psychosomatic illnesses, strange phobias, odd compulsions and a variety of unusual appetites and fetishes. While our conscious ego is focused on how we are doing in the visible external world, these trickster inner energies move about in the murky waters of our unconscious autonomously, following their own agenda. And they can, at times, like Job's leviathan, erupt to overwhelm and swallow our ego whole. They can seize and take possession of us.

Just beyond the reach of our conscious minds are independent energies powerful enough, when aroused, to brush aside our consciously directed willpower. These unconscious energies can cause us to behave in ways contrary to our consciously expressed goals and intentions, compelling us to engage in a variety of unwanted and bizarre behaviors, even to commit suicide---the ultimate crime against our urge for self-preservation!

One cluster of these affect-laden, compulsive energies that roam about in the unconscious consists of the memories and pain of events drawn from our personal histories and experiences that our egos have been unable to integrate into our conscious lives. Particularly during the first third of life, the ego seeks to mold for each of us a separate, unique identity and give us such confidence in our own abilities as will enable us to leave our parents, adapt to the demands and expectations of society at large and achieve such success as will earn us the esteem of our peers.

During this period, the ego is primarily focused on assimilating only such input as furthers these ends. For instance, assume a gym teacher embarrasses a child in front of others by calling him a "klutz" due to a fumbling gymnastic performance. The child's ego may react in several ways. Though consciously aware of the feelings of ineptness and shame flowing from the teacher's overly broad, harsh remark, the ego may refuse to accept the rebuke as factually accurate because of prior experiences which demonstrated to the child that he is not lacking in physical abilities. By such refusal the feelings of ineptness and shame will quickly dissipate and be assimilated and the child's life will move forward as if nothing had happened. Alternatively, however, the child's ego may buy into the accuracy of the teacher's remark and thereby create an inner conflict between the child's need to maintain an image of himself as worthy and competent and the thought that, at least when it comes to physical activities, he is indeed a klutz. Such inner conflict, accompanied by a good deal of anxiety, is likely to manifest itself whenever a choice must be made about playing some sport or engaging in other activities requiring physical skills. In order to avoid such inner conflict and its attendant anxieties the ego may repress the feelings of ineptness and shame and shove them into the child's unconscious. From there, like an unseen oceanic current, such feelings are likely to secretly and subliminally influence the child's subsequent conscious decisions with respect to participation in other activities requiring some degree of physical coordination.

The conscious reasons our egos serve up to justify the choices we make are very often merely rationalizations for what the undertow of our unconscious is demanding of us.

Casting Out Fear

For many of us the most formative of our personal life experiences are our childhood experiences with our parents. When these experiences are positive, we have a good chance of growing up trusting in life's predictability and general supportiveness. When the experiences are negative, we learn to approach life warily, as if it were full of arbitrary uncertainties and hidden pitfalls. And the pain of parental neglect, judgmental criticism, domineering insensitivity or sexual abuse will likely be repressed and relegated to the unconscious. For instance, children often idealize their parents. If a child is then sexually abused by a trusted parent or other relative, the child's ego may push both the memory of the event and its pain into a dark corner of their unconscious. This allows the child to continue to idealize the abusive parent or other relative, thus keeping its whole dependent world from collapsing and their life from coming to a halt.

Sometimes the memory of an event is retained and only its pain relegated to the unconscious. For example, if a child's parents divorce or a parent or close sibling dies, the event may be remembered, but the shock of life's arbitrary unpredictability and the child's intense sense of abandonment and loss may be repressed to allow the ego to keep the child's external life moving forward and avoid his falling into a state of depression.

Still other parental acts may be initially ignored or temporarily forgotten subject to being later recalled. A friend of mine remembers that, when leaving for school during his growing-up years, his parents' standard enjoinder was "make us proud." The parents undoubtedly meant well, but what a lesson in conditional love and what a burden of responsibility to load onto the shoulders of a child!

Because of childrens' limited experience and their long period of dependency and inclination to idealize their parents, they tend to internalize how they are viewed or treated by their parents as being the truth about themselves. For instance, assume a family is riddled with anger and depression due to the alcoholism of one or both of the parents. They are constantly arguing and bickering with each other and often end up shouting at the child. The child receives little supervision and comes and goes pretty much as he pleases and when he does something wrong, the punishment is often disproportionate to the crime.

In such circumstances, the child may nevertheless blame himself for his parents' abusive behavior and attempt to live up to their perception of him as a person of little value, unworthy of their care and concern. He may act out his repressed justifiable anger and fear of abandonment by becoming a rebellious troublemaker, getting his parents' attention by negative behavior and allowing them to escape accountability by making him the scapegoat for the family's difficulties. Or, depending on the bent of the child's character, he may seek to win the parents' attention and save the family's public honor by becoming the mediating peacemaker at home, getting good marks at school and otherwise playing the role of the ever-cheerful, obsessively perfectionist child of whom any parent would be proud.

The point here is that we must dredge up these unconscious, reactive, affect-laden, negative energies—the buried anger and resentments, the fears of loss and not being worthy, the jealousy and envy—derived from our personal life experiences and become consciously aware of their reality and power. Doing so will defuse them of their highly emotional content, take the wind out of their reflexive/compulsive impact on our behavior and integrate them into our conscious lives, thereby keeping them from being so disruptive to us.

Of course another cluster of affect-laden, hidden energies that must be reckoned with and are common to all of us are the existential energies highlighted by Becker and discussed in chapter 1. The very circumstances of our birth, our prolonged period of helplessness and dependency, our self-conscious awareness of ourselves as separate entities who amount to little more than an evanescent mote in the eye of the universe cause us to abandon our awe and wonder about the miraculousness of nature and our own existence. We repress our fears of being overwhelmed by life, of being powerless and insignificant in the cosmic scheme of things. And above all we desperately try to ignore the fact that some day we will die.

Even though we may be vaguely aware of our compensating, compulsive desire for the respect and approval of others generated by our existential fears, it is unlikely that we will ever be able to bring them to the surface of consciousness for any extended period. To do so would bring us face to face with the paralyzing terror of being as nothing! We would risk our lives coming to a halt! But if we are unable to directly confront our existential fears, how are we to discover their existence and confront these shadowy denizens of our psyches and come to some sort of reconciliation with them?

While we may not be able to directly confront many of the repressed energies of the unconscious, such energies, so the psychologists tell us, do speak to us, but only indirectly, in the guise of our emotions and sign, symbol and metaphor. For instance, one mode of expression for such energies is through the symbolic, sometimes mythological imagery found in our nightly dreams. In our dreams, objects, narrative themes and personalities drawn from our rich legacy of myths and folk tales can spontaneously appear mixed up with events and people drawn from our personal lives and histories. If we attempt to interpret this mix of mythological and personal materials literally, the dream seems fragmented and without any meaning. But when interpreted metaphorically, as symbolic, they can often become startlingly coherent.

Take for example the following dreams of a mother and her daughter.[1] The daughter was seven years old and suffering from bronchial asthma, which failed to respond to treatment. There seemed to be no conflict between the daughter and her mother or other members of the family. The girl was intelligent and doing well in school. She seemed to be a model of behavior and obedience. The mother was a school teacher, intelligent but rather cool, under control. And she had a recurrent dream:

I am with a group of women, all masquerading as angels. A man is trying to break into the house, even though all the doors and windows are barred and shut tight. He is an Eastern poten-

---

[1] The following is a paraphrased summary of the analysis of the dreams made by noted Jungian analyst Edward C. Whitmont in *The Symbolic Quest (1969 Princeton University Press).*

tate and he says that if I do not let him in he is going to kill the child.

The daughter also had a recurrent dream:

I am trying to get onto an island from the water, but the goat people or sometimes a huge great goat-man will not let me onto the land, but always pushes me back into the water.

In both dreams the child is in jeopardy. In the mother's dream she is threatened by an Eastern potentate. The mother associated Eastern potentates with despotic, middle-eastern rulers who exploited and used others for their personal advantage. In the child's dream she is threatened by the "goat people" or a "goat-man." In Greek mythology, the minor god Pan has the horns and hooves of a goat. The wild places of the forests and mountains are his home. With his reed pipe he is a playful, gay companion, often engaged in courting the woodland nymphs. He is a god of nature and carefree ecstasy. There is also a horned god in Egyptian mythology--Ammon. He has the head of a ram and is a king among gods, exercising the powers of reproduction, fertility and creation. Both of these gods point to the realm of the instinctual, spontaneous, fertile life. They represent divinities—autonomous energies—which are associated with sexuality, growth and renewal.

Casting Out Fear

Interpreted metaphorically these dreams tell us that there dwells in the mother an Eastern potentate, a proclivity to domineer and control and its converse, an inability to express spontaneity, joy and sexuality, which threatens her daughter's welfare. In the tradition of "mother knows best" and in the name of a sane, proper upbringing, the mother has, with the best of conscious intentions, created an atmosphere of oppressive control in which her daughter is about to drown. The daughter is foundering, finding it difficult to obtain a firm foothold on the terra firma of her own individual identity. Her very breath, her instinctual, exuberant sense of the joy of life, is being squeezed out of her. And this conflict and impasse between mother and daughter is being literally acted out in the symbolic form of the daughter's psychosomatic, asthmatic condition. Her unconscious was speaking to her not only through her dreams, but her illness. After both the mother and the daughter underwent therapy and they understood the hidden dynamics of the energies driving their outward behavior, the daughter's asthma disappeared.

Our unconscious speaks to us in such indirect, metaphoric ways not only through the medium of our nightly dreams but through our daydreams, fantasies and intuitions. It also expresses itself through the projections of our inner lives that are reflected back to us in our folk tales, religions and artistic creations. But it speaks to us most often and loudly through the symbolic language of our emotions. For example, our existential fears and their compensating desires to feel important and valued may bubble up from our unconscious and emerge into consciousness in a variety of derivative emotions.

Embarrassment, guilt, shame and feelings of dependency, inadequacy or powerlessness are the songs of fear. Their flip side includes arrogance, pride, greed, hate and jealousy, the songs of our desire for power, success and esteem. And anger—the great cover-up emotion—may be heard on both sides. These emotions pass through our psyches in an endless collage of various mixes and intensities. They come and go involuntarily, as though a hidden musician were playing the pipe organ of our psyches. Whenever something is said or occurs that causes a rush of anxiety or other strong emotion or impulse to suddenly leap into consciousness, pay close attention because it is probably your unconscious attempting to speak to you.

For instance, if someone makes an unflattering or critical remark about me or questions a decision I have made, my anxiety level and anger rise in a flash as I quickly defend myself, often even before carefully weighing the validity of the criticism or thinking about what emotion or event affecting the other person may have prompted their unkind words. What has really happened here? My flash of anxiety and anger has served as an emotional cover-up for the fact that my self-esteem has been attacked.

For another simplistic example, a friend of mine always shows up with the latest and greatest of everything—cars, sports equipment, you name it. When he would wax rhapsodic in touting to me his latest acquisition, I would attempt to show interest while maintaining what I thought was an appropriate degree of bemused detachment. But one day I accidentally turned the tables on him by acquiring the latest model of a gizmo for which he expressed great admiration and interest. This uncharacteristic upstaging of my friend caused a sudden wave of smug satisfaction and glee to wash over me. And it just as quickly became clear to me that the shield of detached bemusement I had previously put up in such situations was paper-thin and behind it was a good deal of old-fashioned jealousy! It is in such break-through moments when we experience highly charged emotions that our underlying motivations are often revealed to us, provided we are willing to decipher the message.

As noted in chapter 1, much of what occurs in our external lives just happens and we have no control over it. We are born into one historical period or another, into one culture and with one skin color or another. Our families of origin are rich or poor, business people or manual laborers, educated or illiterate. We have no say in the matter. But we tend to hold the opposite view about the thoughts that go in and out of our heads. We believe we are in charge of our thinking and that the application of enough conscious, informed, objective reasoning will reveal the correct answer to virtually any conundrum. We therefore treat the ego's ability to chart a course of action for us as if it was a solely rational process. We seldom recognize or admit to ourselves the degree to which our emotions and their hidden, underlying existential fears and desires provide the direction, the bias for the operation of our rational faculties.

Our ego always has conscious reasons for doing what we do when, *in truth, they are mostly rationalizations for doing what we are unconsciously driven to do.*

When I reflect on my past behavior and the decisions I have made over the years and dig down, asking myself why, why, why I made those particular decisions, I cannot honestly deny that alongside the rational reasons I gave myself for such decisions were other, hidden, often irrational reasons. And these other reasons were mostly derived from an unconscious, compulsive drive to be admired, to appear successful, to be in control and look important!

For example, in preparing a resume some years ago, I listed as my leisure time pursuits such activities as playing tennis, river rafting, fly fishing and hiking. It painted a picture of me as a virile, athletic outdoorsman. But when I reflected on how I was actually spending the majority of my leisure time during this period of my life, I came up with a dramatically different list: relandscaping the backyard; keeping the lawn mowed, the trees and shrubs pruned and the flower beds weeded; painting the children's room; repapering the kitchen; laying a patio, etc. Why? Why all this effort doing things I presumably did not really enjoy in order to achieve only modest changes in the functionality or value of our home but substantially improving its aesthetics? Looking back, I am now convinced that the real motivation for such activities was to look good, to impress our neighbors and friends, to keep up with the Joneses!

For another example: There was a period of years in which my wife and I had expensive season football tickets at a local university, and I would get pretty excited about the games. I would eagerly scan the sports pages for news about the team and upcoming games. Even if I had attended a game, I would look forward to reading news accounts of it the next day and often watched televised reruns of the game. I am up-beat and pleased when the local team wins and a little glum and disappointed when it loses. This excitement defies any rational explanation! It is just a game! It is a non-happening in the cosmic record book! So why, I ask myself, do the games seem so important to me? To say "gee, I just en-joy them" does not explain the emotional energy, time and money I put into them. I believe that, like the spectators of old drawn to Rome's Coliseum, my exhilaration and interest in the games was rooted in the competition, the thrill of the chase and, most of all, the hope of vicariously sharing in "our" team's victory. When *my team* wins, *I* somehow come away a winner, too!

Just reflect on the motivations underlying many of the experiences common to us all:

I just made a smart-aleck quip that got a good laugh. (I feel smugly satisfied with my one-upmanship and being the center of attention.)

I'm all dressed up and ready for an evening on the town or with friends. (My dressing up is not just a matter of showing respect for others. Don't I look sharp? My date or spouse will be impressed. She will be proud to be seen with me.)

And doesn't my date or spouse look terrific? Isn't she a catch? (She is quite a trophy. My friends will be envious. My family will be pleased.)

This new expensive car is really classy and a joy to drive. (And doesn't it make me look rather successful?)

Our new house in this upscale neighborhood will provide more room for our family. (And doesn't it also demonstrate that I am moving up in the world?)

Does the advice I just gave to my client make sense and sound intelligent? (It is not just a question of providing a solution to the problem at hand. It's important to my image, status and success that my colleagues or client be impressed with my abilities, that I seem knowledgeable and have the situation under control.)

I just became a partner in the firm. (It should result in my making more money and it demonstrates that I am a valuable member of the firm.)

Any credible explanation of my behavior and emotional reactions in the above instances must assume the existence of an underlying, unconscious need to win, to be in charge, to be right, to look successful and, conversely, a fear of being powerless, out of control and not respected or admired.

Once again, we cannot begin to know who we are or what motivates us until we pierce the veil of our cultural conditioning and become consciously aware of our compulsive, affect-laden striving to become a hero in the eyes of others, to be someone who counts. By recognizing this pattern in our behavior, we grant ourselves the opportunity to take back much of the power we have transferred to others by conforming our lives to the beliefs, attitudes and modes of conduct *they*—our family and friends and other trend setters in our cultural milieu—deem proper and correct

Becker was not a therapist. He was an academic and theoretician interested in synthesizing the social/psychoanalytical theories of others. Carl G. Jung was a practicing therapist whose psychoanalytical theories were largely drawn from his experiences with patients in dealing with a wide variety of dysfunctional behavior.

Jung was fascinated by the fact that certain symbols, images and personality types appearing in the artistic creations, mythologies and religions of various cultures often cropped up in the artistic works, mythologies and religions of other cultures, as well as in the dreams of some of his patients who could not possibly be acquainted with their cultural source. From such studies he concluded that our psyches are instinctually imprinted with a limited number of patterns or screens that shape how we view and approach the world around us. Since these inborn patterns are common to all men and women in all cultures, Jung referred to them as "archetypes." Jung saw human life as a playing out of the interaction, often conflicting interaction, between our conscious and unconscious attitudes and associations, particularly our hidden archetypal attitudes. Thus, in his view, the unique narrative of each of our lives works itself out within the framework of a limited number of universal themes common to all humanity.

According to Jung, among the principal archetypal patterns imprinted on the psyches of all of us, regardless of gender, are those of the feminine and the masculine.[2] The feminine archetype is expressed in our dreams and artistic creations in the imagery of that which is cool, wet and dark, such as the moon and the earth, and that which is yielding, receptive and enclosing, such as a room or a cave. In our attitudes and actions, the feminine archetype is characterized by an emotional, visceral response to external events; by a feeling-oriented, practical, down-to-earth approach to

[2] Jung postulated the existence of a number of other unconscious archetypal energies, but it would be difficult for one to become consciously aware of their existence and operation in one's life without the assistance of a Jungian therapist or without becoming extensively exposed to Jungian literature and therefore I have not tried to describe them here.

solving problems rather than abstract thinking; by a compassionate, nurturing protectiveness; by a need to be socially involved with and a desire to hold together, unify and inspire others.

These feminine attributes become manifest in the personality and life of a particular individual in several forms, one of which normally predominates while another operates in the background as a secondary personality. The most common feminine form of psychic functioning is that captured by the image of the "earth mother," the generative, nurturing, protector of the hearth, the guardian of the family. She is drawn to marriage and finds fulfillment in bearing and raising children.

A second form of femininity is that of the capable, resourceful comrade (Brunhilde, the girl next door). She can and likes to do what men do and finds fulfillment in achieving success in the workaday world. Another form of femininity is that of the enchanting young love goddess (Aphrodite, Marilyn Monroe). She is a seductress interested in personal interaction with a man. She is unlikely to commit herself to long-term relationships. Lastly, we have the cheerleading, inspiring muse, prophetess or guide (Sibyl, Dante's Beatrice). She often serves as a mediator between the visible and the invisible, the conscious and the unconscious.

Casting Out Fear

The masculine archetype expresses itself in our fantasies and myths as a sword or spear. In our attitudes and actions, the masculine archetype is characterized by abstract, analytical thinking; by a "can do" attitude and energetic response to events; by taking charge; by striving for accomplishment; by concern for the group as a whole and defending law and order; by a willingness to render judgmental decisions and carry them out even though doing so may disrupt social relationships and lead to conflict.

Like the feminine attributes, these masculine characteristics will express themselves in the personalities and lives of individuals in various forms, one of which will predominate while another operates as secondary personality. The most common of these masculine forms is that summed up in the image of the "kingly father," the law-giving, decision-making leader and protector of the group. Another form is that of the warrior hero (Siegfried). He is a "can-do" go-getter who strives for success in the external world. Next is the eternally young, handsome prince (Don Juan). He is a fun companion and lover, but has difficulty committing himself to long-lasting relationships. Lastly, there is the wise old man (Moses, Yoda) who serves as a teacher, a philosopher, a prophet or guide to the mysteries of life.

Both the masculine and the feminine patterns

of psychic functioning (and therefore our predisposition to behaving in the external world in accordance with such patterns) are unconsciously built into each of us, male and female, in some unique blend of the various forms. But as we emerge from childhood, particularly in cultures operating under the influence of the Western Myth, the masculine mode of functioning (in one or another of its various forms) becomes the dominant pattern of functioning for most heterosexual men, and the feminine mode of functioning becomes the dominant pattern for most heterosexual women. Our conscious egos identify with our dominant mode of functioning. And the *contrasexual* impulses within us (the feminine impulses in men and the masculine impulses in women) are split off and repressed, forming an invisible, underdeveloped personality that is relegated to the unconscious. Thus males generally adopt a macho, competitive cultural role. Their feminine qualities, such as their capacity for being in touch with and expressing their feelings, are deemed a liability, an embarrassment. Therefore they remain stunted and undeveloped. Similarly, heterosexual women tend to submerge themselves in their supportive, nurturing roles as wives and mothers. As a result, their underutilized masculine capacities for independent thinking, assertiveness and taking action in the world beyond their family are suppressed, remain primitive and are pushed further into their unconscious. Thus, we become one-sided and unbalanced, men suppressing their feminine impulses and women their masculine impulses.

I have spent so much time describing in an oversimplified manner Jung's views on the interplay between masculine and feminine archetypal patterns of psychic functioning and behavior because I am struck by their similarity to Becker's "twin ontological motives" or strategies for heroically chasing after esteem. In spite of their many differences, Jung's masculine archetype has a remarkable resemblance to Becker's "sticking-out" mode of behavior. And his feminine archetype has a distinct resemblance to Becker's "immersion in the group" mode of behavior. Jung and Becker further agreed that both of these patterns were genetically embedded in both men and women.

However, as a cultural anthropologist and theoretician, Becker was interested in the broad social ramifications of his synthesis of the social/psychological views of others. He was particularly interested in the need for a new social psychology that would reveal to mankind the degree to which we have unconsciously transferred and given up our freedom and independence to our culture's belief system and its trend setters. He emphasized how adoption of the sticking-out and/or immersion in the group strategies has kept us bound to the treadmill of esteem-seeking heroic behavior. But he did not provide us with any detailed advice on how we might get off such treadmill.

Jung, on the other hand, as a practicing therapist, could not avoid assisting his patients in resolving their masculine-feminine conflicts. He believed in self-healing through the transformation of our thinking. He stressed the need to expand the ego's I-centered focus and become *consciously aware* of the fears, desires and impulses that roam about in our *unconscious* seeking some expression in our lives. When we render such hidden energies conscious we give our ego an opportunity to assimilate them and thereby defuse their impact on our behavior. He particularly emphasized the necessity of more evenly balancing and appropriately utilizing our masculine and feminine modes of functioning. Much of what follows in this chapter constitutes a discussion of how a Jungian therapist might view the conflicting masculine and feminine impulses of a patient in the hope that such discussion my help bridge the gap between Becker's general theories and everyone's real life, every day need to expand their ego's focus to include all their secret phobias, biases, compulsions and intuitions.

According to Jung, if the repressed, stunted, contrasexual impulses relegated to the unconscious are not allowed appropriate expression in our lives, the dominant masculine or feminine attitude may adopt a negative face. For instance, if a woman's archetypal feminine energies are not tempered by the masculine qualities of objectivity and reflective, analytical thinking, her nurturing, protective impulses may operate unrestrained and result in her becoming overly possessive, a pushy, meddling controller—a devouring witch! Similarly, if a man's dominant archetypal masculine energies are not balanced by the feminine attributes of compassionate empathy and understanding concern, it may cause a man to exercise his authority in a power-hungry, arbitrary manner, thus becoming a ruthless tyrant!

Our unconscious masculine and feminine patterns of functioning not only seek an outlet for their expression in our own behavior, but by the projection of such patterns onto others. Our inner idea of what it means to be male or female shapes and colors our expectations of persons of the same or opposite sex. For instance, I previously noted the tendency of children to idealize their parents. This is not just due to their prolonged dependency on or being overly impressed by the parents' ability to perform a variety of feats impossible for the child to perform. Such idealization is also due to their projection onto their parents of the archetypal masculine and feminine images that children carry around in their heads.

These archetypal images form the basis for how children *expect* their fathers and mothers to act. As an example of the power of these projected images, we need only look to the children previously mentioned whose parents have utterly failed them. Rather than give up their idealized images of their parents, such children often continue believing their parents really are as they picture them in their heads. They assume that *they* (not their parents) are at fault for all manner of parental abuse and neglect.

Our cultural conditioning and personal life experiences can also influence and shape our archetypal images of what it means to be a man or a woman. This shaping alters our attitudes toward and therefore our relationships with members of the same or opposite sex. Jung referred to emotionally charged blends of our personal experiences and our archetypal masculine or feminine predispositions as “complexes.” For example, if a man’s childhood experience of his father is that of a domineering, arbitrary, sometimes abusive controller, he will likely develop a warped archetypal image of masculinity. Such a person would be deemed suffering from a father/authority complex. He will project onto all authority figures (schoolmasters, bosses, policemen, officials of all kinds) his distorted inner image of the masculine and treat them with the same distrust and resentment, sometimes even open hostility, he holds for his father. This may render him unable to get along with his superiors at work. They will appear to him as always *on his case* and *out to get him.*

Such a person is likely to complain about not being appreciated for his positive contributions and feel defensive and paranoid about all requests of him, always looking for the secret plot against him. Since this is his image of what it means to be male, he will, in turn, tend to treat others under him at work or in his family in the same domineering, arbitrary manner his father treated him. And it is also likely that he will be attracted to and marry a woman, much like his mother, who is willing to subordinate herself to him and put up with such tyrannical treatment.

A good place to begin overcoming his difficulties would be to examine his life and discover the patterns of behavior he has in common with his father. He may find that he not only over-idealized his father, but he in fact unconsciously stored up a great deal of justifiable anger over his father's treatment of him. Such a discovery would further enable him to finally confront his real conflict: a distorted, negative masculine pattern of attitudes and behavior which is at odds with his unconscious feminine impulses for getting in touch with his true feelings, for trying to walk in his father's shoes to understand what made him the way he was and attempting to work out a more harmonious relationship with him. He cannot resolve the conflicts occurring in his external life until he resolves the conflicts in his inner world. He must assume responsibility, not for his father, but for his own unconscious attitudes and negative reactions, his anger and resentment, and for integrating his masculine and feminine archetypal energies into a more balanced whole.

Or take as another example[3] a man who had a weak and non-assertive father and a domineering, over-protective mother. He grew up without developing a lot of self-confidence, was wishy-washy and unable to stand his ground in the face of someone who was assertive. He was prone to day-dreaming and escapism. He married a woman who, like his mother, dominated the family and kept it organized. To all outward appearances she was a model mother and wife. But she had been sexually cold and indifferent toward him for several years and was having a modest love affair with another man.

The nature of his work required him to be away from home frequently and he used the opportunity to engage in a number of one-night stands almost from the outset of the marriage. Nevertheless, he professed that his wife loved

---

[3] The following is a paraphrased summary of a case study reported by noted Jungian analyst Daryl Sharp in *The Survival Papers: Anatomy of a Midlife Crisis* (1988 Inner City Books).

him and he loved her, that his wife and family meant everything to him and that divorce was out of the question. He was willing to feign a "she's entitled to a little innocent fun" attitude toward her love affair and overlook it. All the same, the man was depressed, confused and unhappy.

In Jungian terms he was suffering from a mother complex. His experience of the feminine as embodied in his overly-protective mother was one of being taken care of, not having to think for himself or be accountable for his actions. His unconscious reaction to this experience was to adopt the mantle of the eternally young prince. He refused to grow up and assume the responsibilities of adulthood and married someone who was, much like his mother, a controlling, emotionally lukewarm but efficient person. This refusal has put him in a terrible bind. Publicly, his persona is that of a devoted family man, but secretly his rakish shadow life keeps him engaged in meaningless, compulsive philandering.

If he can become consciously aware of the patterns in his behavior derived from his family history (how he is much like his non-assertive father and how he chose a wife who resembles his domineering mother), he can recognize the fundamental conflict between the masculine and feminine archetypes as they operate in his life. Again, the bind in his external life is but a reflection of this internal conflict. The problem does not lie with his mother or his wife. He cannot change them. He can only change his *reaction* to them and what they stand for in his inner psychic life.

He must cease depending upon the significant women in his life to take care of him. He must acknowledge the lie of his conscious self-image as a devoted family man and accept accountability for his compulsive, childish philandering. He must grow up and bring into play his underused masculine capacities for rational action, discipline, commitment and conscientiousness, even if it means confronting his wife and taking back the power and control he has relinquished to her.

Once again, if we are to discover our true motivations and therefore our authentic, potential self, we must become *consciously* aware of the existence, reality and power of the shadowy, emotionally-charged energies that move about in our unconscious and cause us to behave compulsively, reflexively:

- The mores, prejudices and attitudes imparted and modeled by our parents and the culture in which we were raised.

- Any anger, resentment or jealousy derived from our personal histories or current experiences with others particularly those arising from excessive parental demands or any parental neglect, insensitivity or abuse during our childhood.

- The patterns of heroic behavior we have adopted to overcome our existential fears: i) striving to be admired and respected, to be in charge, have the last word, be better than others (or express other masculine qualities of behavior) and/or ii) allowing our culture and social niche to dictate our mores and attitudes and immersing ourselves in various roles, such as being a nurturing spouse or parent, conforming ourselves to the public personas of our occupations, becoming loyal members and followers of the leaders of various affinity groups, etc. (or express other feminine qualities of behavior).

An awareness of such energies is a necessary first step to dissipating, integrating or otherwise deflecting their force. By becoming aware of such energies, we can begin to formulate and choose our own values, attitudes and goals and take charge of defining who we may become.

To become consciously aware of the reality of such hidden energies we must recognize the *patterns* in the choices we make. How, in the foregoing example, the husband was acting much like his passive father and chose a wife who resembled his controlling mother and how he allowed the significant women in his life to take care of him while he, like a spoiled prince, engaged in his childish extra-marital affairs. Recognizing such patterns forces us to realize that the choices we make are driven, not solely by the superficial reasons we expressed at the time, but largely by unconscious fears, desires and attitudes which have an agenda all their own. Without an awareness of such patterns, we experience our lives as consisting of a series of unconnected, random events that *happen to us* rather than something that *unfolds from within us*.

The importance of recognizing patterns in the choices we make is illustrated in another example drawn from my own life: after finishing my undergraduate studies in the late 1950s, I spent a year in Far Eastern studies at a large private university in New England with the idea of becoming a history professor. The histories of China, Japan and Korea represented relatively unplowed ground for a historian in those days. I was also drawn to Far Eastern studies by the question of whether someone born and raised in Western society under the umbrella of the Western Myth could truly understand and draw any personally useful lessons from the Confucian/Taoist cultures of the Far East. Could people raised in one or the other of such cultures find a common language that both understood? I was fascinated by the fact that the assumptions and underlying worldviews of these two civilizations were (it seemed to me) so opposite from one another, yet both civilizations had been highly successful.

The mythological mind-set of Western society is dualistic and otherworldly. Human beings are seen as separate entities split off from the universe, occupying a position above other creatures and standing alone, often with arms upraised, attempting to discern the wishes or appease the heavenly gods. In the myths of the West man is an unsettled wanderer and warrior constantly engaged in competitive struggles with strange beasts, rival tribes or the gods above. It is a masculine world. The imagery thrown off by the Western worldview revolves around stark contrasts and conflicting opposites: right and wrong; light versus dark; man against nature; heaven and hell. There are few shades of gray. The West's most widely known symbol is that of the Christian cross whose arms intersect only briefly and lightly before stretching out to infinity along the four points of the compass. There is no hint of balance or inclusiveness in such symbol.

In contrast, the worldview of the Confucian and Taoist societies of the Far East is decidedly "this-worldly." Humans are seen as part of a larger order and their chief purpose in life is to get into right relationship with that order: to get into right relationship with one's ancestors, parents and neighbors; to align oneself with the rhythms and *way* of the universe. There is an emphasis on the duties and obligations owed to others and, in Taoism, there is a stress on simplicity and remaining calm and unmoved by the siren songs of power and wealth. It is a world which much appreciates feminine qualities. The themes common to the philosophical writings and literature of the Far East are those of balance and harmony. Its most widely accepted symbol is the representation of the yang and the yin, light and dark, the masculine and the feminine principles, nestled together, like spoons, in an inclusive circle, operating in harmony with one another.

But after a year of Far Eastern studies, I decided that the professorial life was going to be too introverted and sedentary for me and I enrolled in the University of Washington Law School in Seattle, Washington, not far from my hometown. The picture in my head of my life as a lawyer was modeled on Atticus Finch in Harper Lee's *To Kill A Mockingbird*. I saw myself as assisting others in working through their troubles while making a fair living and being a respected member of the local community. Further, my parents, who were having financial problems, were indicating a reluctance to continue to finance my Far Eastern studies at a private college, but were willing to finance legal studies at a public and therefore cheaper university. Upon obtaining my law degree, I did six months of active duty with the Air Force Reserves and then went to work for several law firms in Seattle. After a few years of trying my hand in various legal fields, I ended up choosing to specialize in wills, probate and estate planning.

Thus, long before I ever heard of Ernest Becker or began to study the works of Carl Jung and others in the psychoanalytic field, I was already, at least subconsciously, wrestling with the problem of how to reconcile a competitive, macho, masculine attitude and lifestyle in the legal world with a need for balance and a less judgmental, less aggressive, more feminine, playful and joyful attitude toward life! And by my choice of specialty within the legal field, I was already dealing, however indirectly, with the problem of death!

With the advantage of hindsight I can now see that the reasons I gave for the choices I made during this period of my life were largely driven by unconscious energies of which I was unaware: a need to prove to my parents that I was deserving of their approval; a desire for the respect of my peers and some measure of success in my profession combined with a need to incorporate into my life a better balance between the masculine and feminine qualities within me.

The Invisible Kingdom

During our growing-up years my younger sister and I trod very respectfully and carefully around our father. Though slightly built and not physically intimidating, he was an autocratic, difficult-to-please, demanding man. He could get red-faced with anger over what we often thought were quite minor breaches of house rules or parental requests. We learned at an early age to respond to such outbursts with an emphatic "yes, sir" or "no, sir." If we sought the reasoning behind doing something he had requested of us, the inquiry itself was taken as an act of insubordination, and the answer was most often a clipped "because I said so." When he took a nap on a Sunday afternoon, we gently opened and shut doors, padded about in stockinged feet and spoke in whispers.

I remember my sister (she about 11 and I around 13) saying something at the dinner table in response to a comment made by our father. She said it in a manner that could have been interpreted as "back talk." Every head snapped upright. After a split second of stunned silence, I looked at my sister and cracked, "You'd better smile when you say that." It was just enough levity to get us through a tense moment.

My father was a small-businessman who built a plant in the late 1940s where he made frozen pot pies (chicken, beef) before the competitive pressures created by the national food processors forced him into processing more marginal kinds of frozen foods. His plant was located several miles from our home, on the other side of the small town in which we lived. He was a workaholic and spent most of his time at the plant. Except for Sundays, he was usually up and gone before my sister and I reached the breakfast table and often returned only after we had left the dinner table. Summer was the busiest time of year for my father, so he scheduled vacations with my mother during the school year, and my sister and I were not included. I do not recall all of us ever taking a vacation together, except for the time he rented a cabin for us on Puget Sound for two weeks at the tail end of a summer. It was only forty-five minutes from our hometown, and he commuted back and forth to work during the week.

My father and I did virtually nothing together. So, as a kid, I had a great deal of freedom to do what I wanted to do. I raised and raced pigeons, built a small rowboat and a canvas-covered canoe, and played several school sports. I explored the fields and streams around my small town, trapping muskrats, hunting ducks and pheasants and fishing for trout and steelhead in the local lakes and streams. I reveled in my freedom. But I also felt that I had "raised myself." When I graduated from high school at age 17 and went off to college in New England, I left home for good. I returned home for summer vacations only to work and save money for the upcoming school year.

I do not recall the words "I love you" ever being uttered between my father and mother. Nor do I ever remember such words being directed by him to me or my sister during our growing up years. And he was not given to praising his children, at least not in front of them. For example, I had always gotten pretty good grades, but my first year in junior high I got an "all–A's" report card of which I must have been particularly proud because I recall excitedly bicycling across town to my father's plant after school to show him the report card. He took a perfunctory glance at it, noted the good grades, handed it back to me and grumbled something about how difficult it was going to be to get my bicycle in the car to get it home. So I rode it home alone.

I was not a rebellious young man, but rather, I thought, a fairly responsible, straight-arrow sort of kid of whom a parent might be proud. By the age of 24 I had graduated from college, done a year of graduate work in Far Eastern studies and then completed three years of law school. Just as I was about to leave for basic training in the Air Force Reserves to satisfy my military obligation, my father declared, in a rather clipped voice, that the military would be good for me because "they will make you do what you are told to do." Was I somehow a terrible disappointment to him? Was he just venting about some mistakenly perceived loss of control over me? I doubt that he himself could have answered those questions.

Such trivial, tiny events that occurred so very long ago—but they have been burned into my memory!

I attribute the distance I kept from authority figures (teachers, policemen, officials of all kinds) while growing up directly to my experience with my father. And I still bristle when I am told what to do in a demanding, officious manner.

But in my late 20s my relationship with my father began to change. By then I had gotten married and settled down to practice law in what seemed to me to be a big city, namely Seattle, which was only thirty miles from my hometown where my parents continued to live. For the first time I had the opportunity to attend social events where I could observe him interacting with his adult friends. It quickly became apparent that, among his friends, my father was not the distant, demanding autocrat he had seemed to be while I was growing up. Rather, he was a mild-mannered, likeable man with a wry, Midwest sense of humor.

I also began to hear from him some stories about his childhood. When he was in his late teens, probably around 17, his father, who owned general merchandise stores in several small farming communities in Nebraska and therefore traveled some, had an affair with another woman in another town which was reported back to his wife, my grandmother. As a result, my grandfather---probably at the request of my grandmother, but on the command of her mother, who lived with them---summarily left the family home. My father *never* saw his father again. My grandparents were divorced not long thereafter. My father and his mother and older brother suddenly fell out of the middle class and became part of the working poor. He told me once about having a nickel in his pocket that he carried around for a week debating all his options on how to spend it. How sad and pathetic a story!

However, my father was a hard worker and managed, with some help from his mother's relatives, to get a college education by working full-time while attending school.

In retrospect I believe he saw his primary role as a parent to be the provider his father had not been for him in his teenage and college years. He seemed to have no role model for how to deal with children other than giving them instructions as to what they *must* or *should* do. The intimate, playful, nurturing, cheerleading aspects of parenting simply escaped him. He just did not know how.

So it was up to me to deal with the suppressed anger and pain caused by my father's autocratic manner, criticisms and cool aloofness. I had to determine what kind of relationship I wanted to have with him. And we gradually hammered out a quite affectionate, loving relationship. It was founded not on a sudden, conscious act of forgiveness by me of the pain he had caused me in my youth (I can still retrieve the pain in an instant), but rather on coming to know another, more pleasant side of his personality, the sympathy I had for him because of his dysfunctional childhood, my gradual realization that he just did not know how he was supposed to act when serving in a parental role, the simple passage of time and a gradually evolving decision to not let the old hurts get in the way of my affection for him. And he clearly wanted a relationship with me. As a result, the pain dissipated and melted away. In his later years we always greeted one another with a hug.

But my relationship with my mother was a different story. While in her late teens, she also lost her father—due to a heart attack, however, not divorce. She sought to attend college, but the Depression took hold and she was forced to leave before completing her sophomore year. In my growing-up years my mother was a stay-at-home mom and wife and served as a buffer between my sister and me and our autocratic father. After my sister and I left for college, my mother went to work as a saleslady in an upscale women's wear shop in a nearby city. This was a perfect job for her as she was a willowy, handsome woman with something of a flair for fashion and very much interested in "looking good." She became a very successful saleslady.

By the early 1960s my father's business was failing and when the owners of the women's wear shop where my mother worked decided to retire, my parent's bought the business. Mom made the buying decisions and was the lioness roaming the sales floor. Dad worked the back room and attended to the books. As you might imagine, this change resulted in a major shift in the dynamics of my parents' relationship. With her newfound empowerment and self-assurance, my mother felt free to deliver herself of authoritative opinions on worldly matters about which she knew little and render personal mini-lectures of the "you should do this" or "you must do that" variety. My sister and I winced at these outbursts and would sometimes get into arguments with my mother over the opinions she expressed. Her friends would just ignore her pontificating and lack of logic, saying, "Oh, that's just your mother."

But I believe a Jungian analyst would have instantly recognized her as a woman whose repressed contrasexual masculine capacities were severely stunted. She never developed her capacity for reflective, analytical thinking or the ability to step back and see the full impact of her words and actions on others. Her feminine side remained wildly out of balance with her negative masculine side.

Within the family at least, she also became a controlling, opinionated expert on anything having to do with style, fashion or etiquette. For instance, she might arrive at my home for a family celebration and begin rearranging the centerpiece on the dining room table, saying in an instructional tone of voice, "Oh no, this should be this way." In many instances she may have been correct in her assessment. But she gave no thought to how her behavior and words might be taken as criticism and infuriate my wife. Or she might comment on what a nice outfit our daughter (her granddaughter) was wearing, except "the horizontal stripes make you look fat." If braced about how unnecessarily hurtful her comment had been, she would likely respond that she was just trying educate her in how to select her clothes, not to criticize her personally.

Nor was I exempt from her nagging opinions on what I should do about eating more healthily, developing an exercise program and raising my children. My mother had many good qualities. She was an energetic, generous, social person quick to come to the aid of her friends. But while my relationship with my father improved as I grew older, my relationship with my mother was more contentious and ran hot and cold until her death.

Chapter 3
THE EGO IN IRONS

Midway upon the journey of my life, I found myself in a dark wood; for I had strayed from the right path and was lost.

Dante from the Divine Comedy

My life came to a stop... There was no life in me because I had no desires whose satisfaction I would have found reasonable... The truth was that life is meaningless... If not today, then tomorrow sickness and death will come (indeed, they were already approaching) to everyone, to me, and nothing will remain except the stench and the worms. My deeds, whatever they may be, will be forgotten sooner or later, and I myself will be no more. Why, then do anything?

Leo Tolstoy in Confession

Although it may occur earlier or later or not at all, it is in our middle years, the years from 35 to 45, we are most likely to suffer a crisis which may become the catalyst for effecting a major course correction in the trajectory of our lives. Acquiring an understanding of the symptoms and causes of the crisis should help us weather the gathering storm.

In my case the onset of a midlife crisis was marked by a period of review and reflection about where my life was going both personally in my relationship with my wife and in my career. I had become vaguely dissatisfied with my career as a lawyer. And my enthusiasm for the constant jockeying for power and perks at my workplace and in society at large was definitely on the wane. The esteem-seeking life that had served me so well for so long still provided me with an occasional high, the feeling of being in charge and important. But the rush and the thrill of the chase dissipated more rapidly now, leaving me with a feeling of emptiness. The rat race of keeping up with the Joneses no longer posed an exciting challenge.

More and more often I found myself putting on my public mask, performing my "act" as an assertive lawyer and social conversationalist with a mechanical listlessness. Somewhere along the way, my sense of who I was had merged with what I did and how I held myself out to the public. I began to feel trapped in my public persona, smothered by the mask of self-confidence tinged with a slight air of superiority that I had so carefully crafted. And a wee small voice would occasionally be heard to ask, "Who am I, really? Am I nothing but this public façade? Behind this mask is there still just a child desperately striving to earn the attention and esteem of others? Is such striving to be the main thrust of my life?

I experienced bouts of inexplicable moodiness. I was able to laugh and giggle, but oftentimes there was little joy in me. The relaxed, spontaneous delight of youth seemed to have left me. My physical vulnerability was brought home to me when, in my mid-30s, I came down with a potentially fatal form of cancer of the lymph system. A good friend who was also a doctor saw the histology slides and told me long after the fact that "those were pretty angry cells, and I gave you about a five percent chance to survive."

I also began to witness friends and members of my family succumbing to chronic illnesses, and a few of them even died. I watched my parents age and decline. When I looked in the mirror each morning, I saw my hair growing thinner and my hairline receding, while the chiseled contours of my face and figure softened and grew rounded and flabby. I discovered wrinkles forming at the corners of my eyes. And I began to grasp, not so much in my head as in my gut, that my inevitable death would render meaningless any heroic aspirations I might have had. Not only was I losing my youthfulness, but somewhere along the way I had lost my dreams and ambition. Something within in me had died. My life had lost its sense of direction.

As reflected in the quote from Leo Tolstoy at the beginning of this chapter, the age-old questions occasionally popped into my head: Is this all there is? Having been called into existence, why do I now feel the world is so indifferent to my presence? Indeed, in light of the eons of evolution, of slow upheaval and gradual subsidence, preceding my brief appearance on this earth, am I not just a momentary mote in the eye of the universe? If life is to end with the stench and the worms, isn't all this jockeying for wealth, recognition, position and power a tragicomedy in the theater of the absurd? In spite of all my earthly pretensions and trappings, am I not truly still just a child, alone and helpless?

A mid-life crisis had taken possession of me! My life came to a standstill!

Among the pioneering psychologists of the 20th century, it is Carl Jung once again who has provided the most thorough analysis of the midlife crisis. According to Jung, among the principal unconscious energies whose seismic rumblings and outward push for expression in our lives are at work in causing our midlife crises are the same contrasexual energies discussed in Chapter 2:

the feminine impulses in a man and the masculine impulses in a woman.

In Western societies the vast majority of men have left the rural, agrarian life that kept them in touch with their families and the rhythms of nature and involved them in the nurturing and raising of children, livestock and crops. They now live in cities, work outside their home and away from their families and have had some education or training beyond high school. Except perhaps for those holding assembly line jobs, they live largely in their heads—figuring out, planning, scheming—how to build, operate or repair an item of equipment, how to resolve a problem with a boss or an employee, how to better organize their day or their business, comply with governmental regulations or minimize taxes.

Their archetypal masculine impulses as reinforced by their cultural conditioning under the Western Myth causes males in our society to heavily rely on and overvalue their thinking, analytical skills while underutilizing and belittling their feminine capacity for emotional connectedness. Since such feminine impulses are unacceptable to the male ego's conscious image of what it means to be a man, they tend to be rejected and relegated to the unconscious.

But in midlife a man's dissatisfaction with his

work, combined with the stirrings of his long-suppressed, latent feminine impulses, may cause him to get off the upwardly mobile escalator. He might take a pass on a proffered promotion or consider changing his career. His daydreams and interests are likely to turn inward, toward home and hearth. He may volunteer to coach one of his children's sports teams or become an active participant in a parent group at his child's school. He may fantasize about escaping to the country and getting in touch with the generative rhythms of nature, perhaps even moving to a small town and becoming a rancher or farmer. He may muse about giving expression to his creative, artistic impulses or providing an outlet for his nurturing instincts by giving his time and talents to others through involvement in activities designed to help those who are less fortunate.

For example, in the early 1990's when I was in my mid-50s and as the last of our children went off to college, I decided that duty and obligation had held me in their sway long enough and it was now my turn to do what I wanted to do. My wife and I bought farm property two hours away from Seattle and built a second home as a weekend retreat and, fulfilling a long-time dream, I planted six acres of apple trees and became a part-time commercial orchardist. A friend who made his living being an orchardist warned me numerous times about the deteriorating economics of the apple industry due to the dramatic increase in the cultivation of apples in the undeveloped parts of the world, but I ignored him and moved ahead with my orchard. However, one day he said to me, in a joking tone of voice, “You know, this is a business. You can’t treat these trees like pets. You can’t go around naming them.” His joking comment brought home to me how out of character it was for me to blithely brush aside facts relevant to what I was doing. I suddenly realized that my insistent urge to become an orchardist was being spurred by a rather romantic view of farming and represented a midlife attempt to get in touch with nature and my more feminine impulses. It was also another illustration of emotionally-toned, impulsive/compulsive behavior revealing the strength of the energies that move about in the unconscious.

According to Jungian theory, if a man ignores the rumblings of the feminine impulses coming from his unconscious, his emotional capacities will likely remain child-like, limited to peevish tirades over unimportant matters, petty resentments and passive-aggressive sulks.

So too, a traditional, stay-at-home woman who has been immersed in her role as a wife and mother may arrive at midlife feeling undervalued and unappreciated. She may now find the housebound role she once embraced with joy no longer wholly fulfilling. She may even find it to be oppressive and isolating. As her children leave the nest a major reason for her being walks out the door and the vacuum is likely to leave her disoriented about what to do with the rest of her life. Having been submerged in her family role for so long, she will no doubt feel somewhat inadequate and hesitant about testing her abilities in the outside world. But urged on by her underutilized, dormant masculine impulses, she may also feel a strong need to assert herself, to acquire an identity separate from the one she has as "Mrs. X" or "Y's mom." She will likely also feel a need to prove that she is competent and capable of achievement in the workaday world. She may prepare for a plunge into the outside world by going back to school for additional training or going after leadership positions in local community organizations.

Or she may ignore the rumblings of the repressed masculine impulses coming from her unconscious and fail to overcome her sense of inferiority about being able to make sound decisions and attain a measure of success in the outside world. But by doing so, her ability to think objectively and analytically is likely to remain stunted and undeveloped. She may become overly judgmental and disparaging of others. Such a woman is a good candidate to become, as my mother did, very opinionated on matters about which she knows very little and, when questioned, become argumentative and dogmatic in defending those opinions.

However, it is increasingly rare for a contemporary Western woman to marry right out of high school, to move directly from her parents' home into her husband's home and become a stay-at-home wife and mother. She is more likely to spend a few years in college and then a few more years living and working in a city away from her parents before getting married and settling down. The immediate post-adolescent cultural experience of both contemporary men and contemporary women has become very similar.

Riding the feminist movement of the 1960s and 1970s, contemporary women fought hard to have the same opportunities for high pay and professional jobs as men. Perhaps the biggest boost for women's careers came with the advent of The Pill in the early 1960s. For the first time in history, a sexually active woman could seriously consider a long-term career. Motherhood became optional. Prior to The Pill women knew that childbearing and motherhood were their inevitable fate. No career could be undertaken without taking into account its probable disruption due to accidental pregnancy. And one can only imagine the number of careers not commenced because of the threat of such a fate.

The Ego In Irons

The cultural sea change effected by the feminist movement and The Pill has resulted in legions of contemporary women undertaking serious, successful careers. Upon reaching their mid to late 30s, their biological clocks force them to address the issue of whether they are going to leave their career in order to have a family. But even if a woman decides to have a family, she and her husband may try to rearrange their lives so that both parents, after a brief leave, can continue to work or the wife may stay at home only until the youngest child reaches school age before pursuing her career again.

One result of this cultural shift is that a woman who has spent most of her adult years chasing after a career may have her identity so tied up with her occupational role that the symptoms of her midlife crisis may be very similar to those of a man. Or, if she has successfully pursued a career for a number of years before taking leave to immerse herself in being a wife and mother, she may be able to return to work with fewer apprehensions and quickly regain her sense of self-esteem and competence. And because of her midlife sabbatical as a wife and mother, she may look forward to renewing her career while her burned-out husband is seeking to move out of his career track into uncharted arenas. Thus, she may have an easier time moving through her midlife transition than he does.

Casting Out Fear

Nevertheless, when a husband and wife undergo their midlife crises at the same time, each seeking to redefine his or her identity, it is inevitable that their marriage will come under severe strain. Most couples, so the Jungian analysts say, initially "fall in love" because of mutual projections. Each of them draws from their own experiences and psyche an image of what the opposite sex should be like and projects such image onto the other person. It is an image which generally does not accurately describe the other person and it almost always overvalues and magnifies their good qualities. A man who has found a woman who fits his projected inner image of what he expects a woman to be will be fascinated by her, drawn to her. He will uncritically praise her for her womanly charms and see her as sexually desirable above all other women. He will feel that she fills some void in his soul and completes him. Similarly, a woman who finds a man on whom she can hang her projected inner image of what it is to be a man will tend to see him as a knight in shining armor who can help her navigate the trials and tribulations of life. She too will feel that he fills some empty place in her soul and completes her.

They see each other as they want them to be, not as they really are. For instance, a man with a domineering, critical father and a submissive, easily brow-beaten mother may find that he has projected onto the woman he marries his inner image of what it is to be a woman, an image substantially drawn from his experience with his mother. Thus, he may be attracted to a woman who, like his mother, is non-assertive, meek and lacks confidence in her ability to navigate the rocks and shoals of everyday life. And such a wife may find that she has projected onto her husband her inner image of what it is to be a man, an image of braggadocio, overconfidence and false competence that compensates for her lack of self-esteem and sense of inadequacy. Such projection may have allowed, even encouraged, her husband, much like his father with his mother, to treat her in a curt, dismissive manner.

By the time these two enter their respective midlife crises, their original mutual projections and motivations for marrying one another are likely to have been worn down by the grind of daily living and no longer provide sufficient reasons for their staying married. The cement that previously held their marriage together will have crumbled into sand.

A man's midlife need to redefine himself, to rebel against the shallowness of a life too narrowly focused on career objectives, his need to be reassured about his continued physical and sexual attractiveness and the awakening of his feminine, feeling impulses may come together and lead him into an extramarital affair. He may express his suppressed frustrations, resentments and fears by projecting them onto his wife, who will then become the external cause of his irritable dissatisfaction and "the witch." And he will probably view his mistress as an understanding, sexually desirable goddess come to rescue him.

His wife, particularly if she has been a traditional stay-at-home wife, may in turn feel smothered by her role as his wife and mother of their children and resentful of her husband's apparent freedom from having to perform routine, boring tasks and his daily opportunity for social interaction. She may further feel unappreciated and undervalued for her contributions to the family. She too may have anxieties about aging and her continued physical and sexual attractiveness. Such resentments, fears and lack of appreciation may be projected onto her husband, who then becomes the external cause for her waspish complaints and "a tyrant." The marriage is under siege!

In both cases, a person once seen as fascinating is now seen as infuriating. They must each ask of themselves: Does the problem lie *in here* with me or *out there* with the other person—has the other person changed or, after years of rubbing against one another, is the other just now being revealed for the irritating person he or she always was? Or could it be that the conflicts, resentments and fears being experienced in one's own inner life have been projected onto the other, thereby painting an unflattering, false picture of the person we once loved? As tricky as answering these questions may be, the answer will likely determine whether the marriage survives.

I first began reading the works of Jung and later Becker as I was stumbling through my own midlife and marital crises. These crises were what forced me to undertake a review of my life. It was in the course of this review that I began to realize the extent to which many of my life choices had not been the result of decisions consciously and thoughtfully made. They were more like knee-jerk reactions driven by the programming provided and instilled in me by the archetypal patterns imprinted in my psyche, by my personal life history and experiences with my family, by my culture and its governing worldview and by my existential fears and desires. Only when I came to such realization did I become aware of the extent to which my life had been controlled by hidden energies and secret agendas. I began to recognize the *patterns* in my attitudes, beliefs and behavior— how much my prejudices resembled those of my family, how much my values mirrored those of the Western Myth, how overly macho I was in my attitude towards women. And I was able to see how much of my life was being lived as a preprogrammed robot.

Chief among these hidden, motivating energies was a need to *count*, to be right, to be admired and respected, to be deemed a success in the eyes of my family and friends and my professional peers. I was practically a poster child for a person in pursuit of the esteem of others. Becker had described me quite accurately! And I was so slow in recognizing it because so many around me were doing the same thing.

But having arrived at my middle years, I found the esteem-seeking lifestyle not nearly as seductive as when I was younger. I also felt like I had become trapped in a squirrel cage of duty and obligation. My life, it seemed, consisted of busily rushing about trying to live up to my public persona and proving myself to others. I was often reminded of the sad lament of George Babbitt, Sinclair Lewis' fictional icon of mainstream, conformist America: "I've never done a single thing I've wanted to in my whole life."

Further, I had always prided myself on a degree of dogged perseverance (some would call it Dutch stubbornness) in analyzing and solving problems, but as hard as I tried, I could not seem to get any resolution of the issues that kept popping up over and over again between myself and my wife. I began asking myself with ever greater frequency if I wanted to stay married to her and continue to live like I had been lo these many years. And the answer always came back the same. So at the age of 47, after feeling I had made a solid effort to salvage our marriage of 20 years, I initiated a parting of the ways. I did so with much reluctance and great concern for our two children. And unfortunately our divorce was not amicably resolved.

To go through a contentious, litigated divorce and a midlife crisis at the same time is a stressful, confusing and humbling experience!

Chapter 4
FROM HERE TO ETERNITY

Man wants to know that his life has somehow counted, if not for himself, then at least in a larger scheme of things, that it has left a trace, a trace that has meaning. And in order for anything once alive to have meaning, its effects must remain alive in eternity in some way.

Ernest Becker in *Escape From Evil*

The decisive question for man is: Is he related to something infinite or not? That is the telling question of his life... If we understand and feel that here in this life we already have a link with the infinite, desires and attitudes change.

Carl G. Jung in *Memories, Dreams and Reflections*

To recap a bit, each of us arrives on earth alone and naked, looking up in awe and wonder, as a vast, majestic and overwhelmingly powerful world swirls around us. Our self-conscious sense of set-apart-ness, cosmic insignificance and impotence and the gradual realization that in a few span of years we will die generates such anxiety and terror that we deny and repress the truth of this reality. To compensate, we take up the sticking-out and/or the immersion in a group modes of heroic behavior. Such modes of behavior give us the illusion that we are not insignificant and powerless, but rather we are special and superior to others and therefore our lives have a measure of cosmic importance. Such illusion allows us to delude ourselves into thinkingl that when we die, some trace, some mark of our existence will continue into eternity.

As more thoroughly described in Chapter 1, the sticking-out style of heroics requires that we strive to earn the admiration and respect of others by being better than they are at some skill or profession, by becoming wealthier or otherwise earning more badges of success than possessed by our peers. By demonstrating such superiority we earn their esteem, become a hero in their eyes and make it possible that we will be remembered long after our death, thereby attaining a small degree of immortality. At the other end of the spectrum, the immersion in the group style of heroics requires that we surrender our uniqueness, submerge ourselves and take our identity from one or more of the religious/political/social groups active in the culture in which we live. If the group claims its members are somehow special because of their religious tradition or ethnic or racial heritage, it taps into the need of its individual members to feel special, important and superior to others. And by membership in such a group, we become participants in a larger order that will carry on the tradition or heritage represented by the group after we are gone.

The sticking-out and the immersion in the group modes of heroic behavior are the means by which we create the illusion that we are better, more successful and superior to others. They are the twin pillars supporting our unconscious search for immortality. As a male born in America just prior to World War II and weaned under the influence of the Western Myth, and by virtue of the nature of my character, I gravitated early on to the sticking-out style of heroics.

But as I moved through my middle years, my enthusiasm for the constant jockeying for position and chasing after achievement and success began to wane. It became increasingly apparent that, as inescapable as adoption of the sticking-out, esteem-seeking lifestyle may have been in my youth, it was providing me with fewer and fewer highs. The ability of such a lifestyle to give me a sense that I was living a meaningful and purposeful life was in serious doubt. I felt like I was frantically treading water. My head occasionally took in the air that intoxicated me with the idea that I was special, better, even superior. But my weary body was telling me that my challengers were about to overtake me and that I was near to drowning in my manic efforts to earn society's attention and esteem. The harder I struggled to stay afloat, the lower I sank.

In the end, chasing after the esteem-seeking lifestyle proved to be a fraud. The sticking-out mode of heroic behavior asks that we seek the esteem of others by being better; by acquiring more fame, power and wealth than they have; *by setting ourselves apart and above them.* Such striving only served to accentuate and reinforce my sense of lonely set-apart-ness! Moreover, as Jung would have been quick to point out, it is a one-sided, masculine lifestyle emphasizing judgmental intellectualization, action and the exercise of authority and control, sometimes to the point of abuse, mistreatment and exploitation of others. It is a lifestyle too often lived on the blustery battlefields of sharp words, organizational intrigues, puffery and hype.

We even find many women (who, by their natures, have a greater capacity for intuition, play and the nurturing of relationships) who nevertheless feel that to be successful in the workplace they must be as cut-throat, ruthless and unreasonably demanding as they suppose successful men are.

It breeds friction and conflict. It is a lifestyle that alienates us, not only from others, but often from ourselves and our repressed contrasexual impulses (a man's feminine impulses and a woman's masculine impulses). And it does not provide a bridge across the abyss that separates the ego-centric, self-conscious *me* from *thee* and the universe beyond. Rather, it isolates. Further, it keeps us from facing up to the reality of our true existential situation and seeing that, in spite of whatever successes we may have here on earth, we are *all* equally insignificant and powerless in the cosmic scheme of things. It impedes our acquiring humility. While it may allay our existential fears, the sticking-out mode of heroics does not enable us to confront and reconcile ourselves to the reality of our existential situation in a manner that not only calms our terrors, but leaves us feeling at peace and contented. It does not bring us together or make us whole.

But what about the immersion in a group mode of heroics? Will submerging our lives and conforming to the beliefs, values and expectations of the various religious/political/social groups spawned by the culture in which we live quiet the terror generated by our existential fears and enable us to confront those fears with equanimity? Will it give us the feeling that the group (and, vicariously, each of its individual members) is of cosmic significance? Can it lead us to a sense of peace and contentment?

As previously touched upon, man, ever ingenious, has fabricated numerous elaborate religious/political/social belief systems designed to provide a sense of togetherness, self-worth, importance and participation in a greater order of life that will outlive and thereby confer upon us a link to the infinite. By conforming to its ideals, values and attitudes, by distrusting our own independent judgment and giving uncritical support to the schemes of its leaders for the group's aggrandizement, its members are made to feel they are valued participants in the group's success. The group will preserve the ideological legacy and carry on the success of its current members long after they are gone, thereby assuring the departed members a measure of immortality and cosmic significance. Such assurance renders the group's belief system sacred to its members. It becomes—whether or not they label it as such—a *religion.* And its members will defend it with their lives!

Joseph Campbell describes this process of transcending our fear of death by reaching out to the eternal through immersion in the group as follows:

> Not only does the individual member of our species, conscious of himself as such,

> face death, but he confronts also the necessity *to adapt himself to whatever order of life may happen to be that of the community into which he has been born, this being an order of life superordinated to his own, a superorganism into which he must allow himself to be absorbed, and through participation in which he will come to know the life that transcends death.* (Emphasis added.)

The emergence of patriotic nationalism, Hitler's national socialist fascism, communism and, more recently, the rise of militant Islamic religious fundamentalism are all examples of culturally defined attempts to attain cosmic significance by means of immersion in a larger group. What is the appeal of these belief systems? What draws us to them? Each has as its central psychic attraction a dream-like utopian vision of individuals coming together and marching off in lockstep to defend against some threat or accomplish some task that will preserve the group's heritage, prestige or power and assure its survival into the future. The "isms" have held us, by the millions, in their power by virtue of their connecting us with one another and the promise that the faithful, the people, the nation, the group so united under one banner will survive the death of its individual members and endure forever. The allure of the isms is founded on the assurance given their followers that their lives, in the words of Becker and Jung cited at the beginning of this chapter, will have left a "trace" in "eternity" and are "related to something infinite."

The isms further beguile us because they have tapped that vein in us derived from fear, that is, our need to stand out, be better, more powerful and superior to others, not just individually but collectively. Those operating under the sway of one of the isms are continually reminded of their importance to the *cause.* They are treated as heroes.

Patriotic nationalism's usual form involves a civilian population coming to a consensus and uniting behind its leaders in support of a military effort of defense or expansion. People are urged to rally to the flag—the symbol of the group. Sacrifices are called for in the name of preserving the motherland, the fatherland or advancing the collective's manifest destiny. Those who die for the cause are promised that their deeds will be engraved in stone, recounted in song and long remembered.

Hitler's fascism offered to lead Germany out of the political turmoil and economic chaos surrounding the disintegration of the Weimar Republic, to unify the nation, purify it of foreign influences and establish an enduring, thousand-year Reich.

Casting Out Fear

Communism averred that out of the dialectics of class struggle and historical necessity, the working masses were destined to gain control over the means of production. Uniting together and working shoulder to shoulder for material progress, the workers would lead communism's believers into a classless, utopian era where each was to perform according to their ability and receive according to their need.

Militant Islamic religious fundamentalism seeks to turn back the historical clock to establish clerically led caliphates across the Muslim world (combining both religious authority and political power in a very few hands) in order to cleanse it of Western materialism and other degenerate Western social influences. The militants wish to reinstate sharia, the divinely inspired strict code of conduct that regulates not just religious practices but all aspects of human activity. America is viewed as the principle source of such evil Western influences and therefore the *Great Satan*.

But just as our attempt as individuals to stick out, to rise above our peers, fails in the end to overcome our sense of set-apart-ness and bring us together, so the immersion of our lives in a larger group (however much it aids us in repressing our existential fears) also betrays and fails us. In fact, the sticking-out mode of cultural heroics usually involves action by only a single individual.

Therefore, the harm (abuse, exploitation, killing of others) that may be inflicted pursuant to this mode of heroics is necessarily limited to the unfortunate few who come in contact with the single individual who operates under its sway. But when we immerse ourselves in a group that engages in harmful behavior, because of the sheer number involved and the ability of its leaders to focus its larger energies and resources, the harm that can by inflicted on others is immensely magnified. And as the history of the 20th century has demonstrated only too clearly, the isms have a terrible, sadistic, dark underside: They require victims! Scapegoats! They have led to violence against our fellow humans on a genocidal scale!

The nationalistic patriot is told by the nation-state that the enemy is not just misguided but evil, an abomination that must be excised and crushed into dust, forever obliterated. And those who fight in the cause of saving society from such an enemy will be admired and respected, treated as heroes, as saviors. Those who sacrifice their lives for the cause will be raised up and immortalized.. Their deaths will be mourned by many. Their deeds will be long recounted in song and verse, and their names placed on monuments.

Hitler's fascist preaching's resonated with the German people's need to feel proud again after their ignominious defeat in World War I. Hitler assured them they would rise in glory again, become a "master race" and dominate the world. But a condition of such domination was removal of the threat posed by an imagined conspiracy of "international Jewry" and the blood taint of the "Jude."

Communism was infected by the idea that the dialectics of history gave the industrial masses the right, not only to seize power but to exterminate dissenters and self-righteously impose their system on others.

The militant Islamic fundamentalists have little tolerance for other religions and preach, as did Hitler, a virulent, exterminatory form of anti-Semitism. As backers of Israel and being mostly of the Christian faith, Americans are seen as heirs of the Crusaders who should be killed wherever they may be found. The Islamic fundamentalists do not hate the West because they are suffering from the *oppression* of Western colonialism. Except arguably in Palestine, the West turned over their colonies to indigenous control and withdrew from the Muslim world decades ago. Muslims hate the West and Israel in particular because they suffer from a sense of defeat and inferiority that can be wiped away only by blaming others and killing the *infidels*. They see themselves as victims defending their faith and their honor.

So, in the name of all that is good and pure, we engage in genocidal evil. Ordinary good people become, not just the willing but the *eager* instruments of such evil. In the grip of their primal fears, enthralled by the supposed superiority of their worldview or feeling that their belief system is under severe attack, they become imbued with false pride and arrogant self-righteousness and cease to see the other side as much like themselves. When we disparage, discount and look down upon the racial, ethnic or cultural backgrounds of others, when we attack their religious/political/social beliefs and values, we threaten what is sacred to them, the *very core of their existence*.. We raise in their minds the terror-producing possibility that their cultural belief system may be wrong.

We confront them with the terrible prospect of losing the cultural armor that has validated them as special and important, boosted their esteem and kept them from facing the reality of their existential situation and their primal fears of estrangement, insignificance and mortality. The meaningfulness, *the very raison d'etre of their lives,* is at stake! Naturally they rise in anger to strike back in fierce defense of their worldview and their honor. Is it any wonder that religious and political discussions generate so much heat and so little light? That differences in religious/political/social beliefs have led to so many conflicts over the centuries? That so many people have willingly, eagerly laid down their lives asserting or defending the truth of their various cultural belief systems?

When we become corrupted by our belligerent self-righteousness with respect to our own cultural belief system, we demonize our enemies. They become the "foreign devils." And we become the power-wielding, abusive, unfeeling robots we accuse our enemies of being. Worshipping at the altar of the mass modern state has resulted in our personally witnessing within our own lifetimes many of the most monstrous mass crimes of recorded history. Our organized religions have been all too often misled by smug self-righteousness into becoming the perpetrators or supporters of vile terroristic crimes and armed struggle.

Our historical experience with the isms and other belief systems has been that, in the heat of battle, it is nearly impossible for a society to maintain its balance on the high wire of brotherhood, compassion and forgiveness. Marching in lockstep under the banner of truth and justice and unconsciously grasping for esteem and immortality, they almost always cause us to fall into prideful arrogance and malignant vindictiveness, destroying lives and tearing apart the social fabric of our supposed enemies to a degree far greater than is required just to win the battle. The isms may unite us with members of our own group, but they ultimately fall short and fail us because they do not embrace all people, all of life. They are aimed at unifying, raising up and guaranteeing the survival of only one particular social class, one specific ethnic, racial, political or religious group or one particular nation. However effective immersion in a group may be in allaying our existential fears, such style of heroics, just like the sticking-out mode of heroics, has failed us. Both lead to friction and conflict. Neither has led us to a sense of peace and contentment.

Thus, in Becker's view the violence that humans have inflicted on their own kind over the centuries is attributable, after all other explanations, to humanity's intense need to be respected and admired, to occupy a position of power and control, to feel more successful, more virtuous and otherwise superior to others. These are all needs generated by our existential fears of insignificance, helplessness and mortality. As those of us born in the 20th century know only too well, human striving for esteem and power has often led to conflict, class warfare, civil wars and even genocide, particularly with respect to those who do not share our own cultural worldview.

However, Becker would also agree that not all heroic activities are as destructive as the isms.

Being known as a good provider or a solid citizen or devoting one's life to more altruistic purposes, such as finding a cure for cancer or marching for civil rights, can provide a measure of deserved self-esteem without putting down, exploiting or harming others.

Within a few months of being separated from my first wife, it became obvious to me that I enjoyed being married. Not because, as I was chidingly accused, I needed someone around to cook and clean and make my bed, but because I enjoyed the camaraderie and repartee that goes on between a loving couple. The legal advice I ordinarily gave to divorce clients was to remain single and not remarry for at least two years so that they could become entirely comfortable living alone. Only then could they make an intelligent decision about whether to risk bringing a new person into the midst of their daily routine. But within six months of my own divorce, I met and married a woman who had been divorced several years earlier. I was blessed with a stroke of incredible luck: she has been my best friend and soulmate ever since!

She had custody of her two boys, both of whom had been adopted, and shortly after our marriage my two children, a girl and a boy, also came to live with us. So while my new wife and I were sorting out how to live with one another, we were also trying to bring some order to the chaos created by four children ranging in age from nine to sixteen. As you might expect, her children resented the "new guy" and did not take kindly to taking orders from me. Nor did my children like taking orders from her. Neither did the children like being forced to live in the same household with one another.

We had no inkling how difficult it was going to be to blend all these preteen and teenage personalities, especially with two ex-spouses/parents hovering in the background who did none of the heavy lifting in raising or disciplining the children and to whom a child could run when feeling aggrieved by having to follow the ground rules at our house. We both had full-time day jobs. But when we came home each evening it felt like we were returning to our nighttime jobs! One or another of the kids always seemed to be outspokenly or sullenly angry or upset about something. We curtailed our outside activities to focus on issues with our children. But we survived, all of us—and eventually we became a family!

While my new wife and I tried to bring some order and peace to our new household, I continued to work on "my issues." Even though I realized that the sticking-out mode of heroic behavior was failing me, I did not (and probably couldn't even if I had wanted to) completely abandon my pursuit of the esteem-seeking life. The need to do so was deeply ingrained in me. Also, from a financial point of view and even though most of my legal work came from referrals from other professionals, to sell services as personal as legal services I needed to remain involved in the community and various bar committees and keep selling myself as a competent, knowledgeable lawyer. A little suspender snapping was good for business no matter how much I disliked doing it. But I did temper and lower the intensity of my pursuit of the esteem-seeking lifestyle.

I began devoting more time to my new family and doing things that were a genuine expression of what I wanted to do. I turned down several offers to serve or continue to serve on boards and committees. I volunteered to coach my sons' boys' club basketball team. I became more involved in my children's school activities. I made a greater effort to be a good listener, to be more aware of who I might offend when I spoke out on a matter, to pick my fights over issues more carefully. I also began to reexamine whether my political allegiances and views needed to be modified and rebalanced.

Chapter 5
THE BIBLE AS METAPHOR

In the beginning God created the heaven and the earth.

Genesis 1:1

Becker's own view of his contribution to social/psychoanalytical science was that his synthesis of the theories of Freud, Rank and others had brought such science to the point of merger with the Judeo-Christian religious tradition.

According to Becker's synthesis of such theories, the circumstances that accompany everyone's arrival on earth---a self-conscious awareness of our cosmic insignificance, powerlessness and mortality---generates intense anxiety and fear. As a result, we deny the reality of such circumstances and compensate therefore by adopting a lifestyle and culturally defined worldview designed to impress others with our wealth, fame, power or other indicia of our individual superiority and/or we submerge ourselves in a racial, religious, ethnic or other larger, on-going group that makes us feel as if we are special and among the anointed. We behave in such ways to create the illusion that we are somehow better, more superior than others and therefore our lives have a measure of cosmic significance.

The Judeo-Christian theologians paint a similar picture of the human condition. They begin with the proposition that mankind is inherently flawed, that is, we are prone to selfishness and disobedience and therefore easily tempted into obsessively chasing after wealth, fame and power. Like Becker, the theologians assert that striving for such goals creates only a this-worldly illusion of status and importance, that they are "false gods" which cannot lead us to the paradise that is the "kingdom of God." And the theologians have a ready answer for how we may escape from the grasp of our obsessive pursuit of such heathen "idols:" we must transform our thinking, that is, repent---come to a new understanding---of our evil ways, pledge allegiance to the God the Bible, humbly ask for His mercy and forgiveness and follow His commandments.

Similar to the theologians, Becker also asserted that the only way mankind could escape from the squirrel cage of chasing after wealth, fame and power is by finding a link to a "religious dimension," a connection to some larger, higher power.

Thus, said Becker, has modern social/-psychoanalytic theory dragged mankind up to the door of religion and dropped it on its doorstep!!

Sooo---if I was going to find my way out of the labyrinth of confusion and doubt of my middle years, apparently, according to Becker, I had to pass through the doorway of some sort of religious awakening and refocusing of my life. It was with great reluctance that I approached such portal. In fact the most protracted and fiercest debate I have ever had with myself has been over the issue of religion.

For years I sat in the hard pews of the Episcopal Church intellectually stewing and fuming, trying to find some way of understanding the strange words that kept crashing around me. Come listen with me.

First, in the Apostles' Creed, we are asked to swear to the truth of certain factual propositions:

> I believe in one God, the Father Almighty, maker of heaven and earth and of all things visible and invisible….

How incredible! Are we not being asked, on oath, to believe that there is another reality, an invisible world *out there*, a spirit world of angels and archangels presided over by an intangible *someone* or *something*, some energy/being called God? Are we not being asked to believe that this

Casting Out Fear

God has single-handedly created everything in the universe, including the complex creature known as man? Are we expected to take this statement of fact at face value, as the literal truth?

Next we are enjoined to acknowledge that we are an innately sinful lot:

> Most Holy, we confess to you, to one another, to the whole community of saints in heaven and earth, that we have sinned... We have been deaf, blind, indifferent. We have not been true.

This God has apparently given humans some degree of free will, but at the same time endowed us with a nature predisposed to sin. Why would an all-powerful God do such a thing?

And then, amazingly, we are told to look to this same God for the forgiveness of the acts that flow from our sinful natures:

> Our heavenly Father, in His great mercy, hath promised forgiveness of sins to all those who with hearty repentance and true faith turn unto Him...to the end that all that believe in Him should not perish but have everlasting life...

Can this be? Does this invisible, formless *some-*

one or *something* out there even know of our existence? Or take a personal interest in each of us? Love us in spite of our errant ways? Will He relieve us of our pain and suffering? Enable us to enter the peace of paradise? Even give us eternal life? Oh, where are you now! Show yourself!

Then:

> (Being handed the wafer): Take. Eat. This is the body which has been given for you. (And being offered the cup of wine): Also drink ye this. Drink this in remembrance that Christ's blood was shed for you.

Such words fall on my ears like some mystical incantation from a forgotten cult of a lost civilization. My skeptical, scoffing mind wants to dismiss them out of hand.

Strangely, the Bible never gives us a direct description of this *someone* or *something* called God. Rather, it portrays Him[4] indirectly through images of His powers and a few stories showing Him in action. In these images and stories He is depicted as an invisible, formless, supernatural, *someone* or *something* who exists *out there*, be-

---

[4] I refer to God in the masculine forms of pronouns for convenience purposes only.

yond and outside of the natural, physical world composed of the planet Earth and the heavenly bodies swirling about us. We are told nothing of His origins or how He came to be. He is apparently an uncaused cause, born of himself.

Among the principal stories depicting God in action is the creation story set forth in Genesis in which we are told that He created the whole of the universe. First, He created all the heavenly bodies, including the planet Earth. Then he created all the plants and animals, endowing them with life. Lastly, he created humans: first the male, Adam, from a handful of dust and then, from his rib taken while asleep, the female, Eve.

Adam and Eve lived in idyllic innocence and ease in a garden of harmony and plenty known as Eden in which stood the tree of eternal life and the tree of knowledge of good and evil. They were specifically enjoined by God not to eat the fruit of the latter tree. One day, tempted by Satan in the form of a snake, they disobeyed the command of God and ate the forbidden fruit, became self-conscious and covered their nakedness. For their disobedience, God banished them from Eden to a life of difficulty and drudgery tilling the soil. They were further sentenced to being mortal, to a limited life span and then returning to the earth they were condemned to work. A guard with a flaming sword was posted around the tree of eternal life to prevent them from returning to the garden, eating its fruit and regaining immortality.

I stand in awe of the marvelous diversity of nature's life-forms---its animals, insects, fish, birds and plants—and the astonishing array of adaptations they have made to survive in a multitude of environments. But I am especially awed by the creature known as man, a creature which has been given a self-conscious awareness of himself as separate and apart from all other things and a capacity for reason, memory and imagination unknown among nature's other creatures. But as an explanation of the origins of the universe and the life-forms that occupy it, I find the creation story of Genesis lacking in credibility. I cannot conceive of an invisible, formless, someone or something which could have *single-handedly designed and created* the many varieties of atoms and molecules that make up matter, invented the intricate rules of biology, chemistry, electricity and physics that govern their interaction, endowed a portion of such matter with the ability to subdivide and replicate itself in an exploding extravaganza of life-forms and then crowned it all with the creature we call man. My imagination is just unable to hold in its grasp the concept of a single designer, an evanescent, supernatural someone or something (born of itself?) that could possess such enormous and sustained creative powers and inventive intelligence.

Genesis' single designer theory of the origins of the universe seems to me further belied by the amount of unpredictability, randomness and instability that remains operative in the universe. If a single designer was trying to bring some order out of chaos in piecing together the universe in a more organized fashion, why leave so much undone?

Also, scientific advances in our reading of the rocks and bones, in our observations of the heavenly bodies and our studies of the inner structure of atoms are bringing us ever closer to a more intelligible understanding of how the universe works. Thus, as an explanation of our origins, I believe at least a substantial minority of Western society today, including me, would agree with Pierre Laplace, the 18th century French astronomer, that the "God hypothesis" is no longer intellectually needed or defensible to fill in the gaps in our knowledge and understanding of the universe. The God hypothesis has simply ceased to have any relevant value for us.

Furthermore and leaving aside for the moment the credibility of the many miraculous events reported in the Bible (virgin birth, resurrection, walking on water, etc.), there is the more important issue of an all-powerful God who permits the innocent to suffer pain and injustice. A literal reading of the Old Testament shows God as all-powerful and all-knowing. He is pictured as a rather cold, judgmental, father-figure who demands that we acknowledge Him as our sole god, submit to His power and influence and conduct ourselves righteously, in accordance with His commandments. If we do so, He promises to cause us to wax prosperous, to protect us from our enemies and enable us and our fields and flocks to survive disease, pestilence and drought. The degree to which we share in such beneficence or suffer His punishments depends on how well or poorly we conduct ourselves.

In the New Testament, God is depicted as a much warmer, more hands-on, loving mother-figure who is far more inclined to forgiveness and mercy than the God of the Old Testament. Conduct offensive to Him may not immediately result in the imposition of punishments, but may be forgiven, provided one acknowledges His supremacy and turns to the path of righteousness. God's revised covenant with mankind is that not every misstep will condemn us to hell, that He loves us in spite of our frailties and that His mercy and entry into heaven are still available even to those who have wandered from the path of righteousness, provided they sincerely repent. Unlike the Darwinian God who sets the world in motion and then stands back to watch, the Biblical God takes a personal interest in us. We are told that He loves every one of us just as fathers and mothers love their children. As a shepherd watches over his flock, so God watches over us. He shares in our pain and listens to our prayers.

The more fundamentalist Christian would put it even more fervently. He would tell us that God so loves us that He became incarnate in Jesus Christ in order to deliver to us His message of love, forgiveness, reconciliation and eternal peace. He would further say that, through His son Jesus, God suffered for us, shed His blood and died for us.

God is not only portrayed as a personal, loving god, but also as a god of social justice. The Bible exhorts us to look after the widows and the orphans, the poor and the lame—all the outcasts. We are to turn the other cheek, love our enemies and do unto others as we would have them do unto us. Those who look after their neighbors can expect to receive His bounty. Those who do not can expect to be struck down.

Implicit in the idea of an all-powerful, all-knowing, personal God who loves each of us and is concerned with social justice is a commitment to exercise His enormous powers to intervene in human affairs to relieve suffering and do justice.

But from the vantage point of contemporary times, what is God's track record for benevolent intervention in human affairs?

When we examine the Bible closely and look, not to God's words but to His actions, we find Him intervening only minimally in human events and even then, seemingly, not always rewarding the faithful or coming down on the side of justice. In the book of Job, on a wager with Satan as to the strength of Job's faith in Him, God stood by and allowed Job's children and servants to be slaughtered, his herds stolen and Job himself to be stricken with painful boils.

Unaware of the wager, his friends insisted that Job must have committed some acts villainous enough in the eyes of God to deserve such punishment. They assumed that God would not intentionally allow Job to suffer so. To assume otherwise would require them to abandon their belief in the existence of a beneficent covenant between an all-powerful God and humanity. But Job was adamant that he had committed no such villainous acts and demanded some justification for his mistreatment, some answer to the question of why, if God loves us, the righteous must suffer. Without the slightest twinge of moral consciousness for having goaded Satan into subjecting Job to such torment, God evaded the issue, shouting out of the whirlwind:

Casting Out Fear

> Where wast thou when I laid the foundations of the earth? Shall he that contendeth with the Almighty instruct Him?

Intimidated by God's bluster and vague suggestion of some secret design apparently never to be revealed to man, Job wilted:

> Behold, I am vile; what shall I answer thee? I will lay mine hand upon my mouth.

When we look outside the pages of the Bible to the experience of most of us in modern times, we search in vain for evidence of something *out there*, above and beyond the natural universe, that loves us, that personally cares for us and dispenses beneficence among us in accordance with the degree to which we deserve it. Our scientists have sent their instruments into the far corners of our galaxy and peered into the universe beyond, only to confirm that, so far as we can yet determine, it is a barren, hostile place. Only down here on the planet Earth have the narrow conditions (air, water, limited temperature extremes) necessary for life as we know it been produced.

And the history of mankind on this verdant sphere has been a sad and lengthy litany of the death and destruction wreaked by war, disease and natural calamities; the hardships imposed by tyrannical political systems and the cruelties sanctioned by social systems based on caste, class and color. Those of us coming to maturity in the 20th century have been personal witnesses to many of the most outrageous mass crimes ever recorded: the systematic extermination of large segments of various populations—the Jews, Kulaks, Cambodians, Ruwandans and others—and the personal indignities and economic hardships of racial, ethnic and class injustice in the United States, Africa, India and elsewhere. We have seen the crippling or death of millions of innocent children by starvation and disease.

In our personal lives we have been present during long and painful illnesses followed by the premature deaths of deserving friends and members of our families. And we all have participated in the pain and dislocation that comes from just the everyday forms of bad luck: being laid off from one's job, suffering a disabling injury, the loss of a crop due to flood or drought. Yes, we are also witnesses to occasional occurrences of beneficial events and instances of inexplicable good luck. But just as often we see the decent, the considerate and the generous go unrewarded and bear more than their share of human suffering while the manipulative, the greedy and the corrupt rise to prominence, power and wealth. There is no rhyme or reason to it. We cannot explain away such a massive, long-term record of pain, suffering and loss on the basis that those who suffered were so inherently evil and unrepentant that they *deserved* such a fate or that those who escaped such treatment were not deserving of the same fate.

If this God *out there* is as all-powerful as He is depicted in a literal reading of the Bible but will not tear aside the veil that separates Him from us, if He will not reach out to give us a hand and help relieve the suffering and injustice that is a birthright of many of us, then whether or not He exists or loves us becomes a matter of indifference. With such a record of non-intervention and neglect, who can continue to believe in a divine, loving providence? Who can believe that some ethereal energy/being, that someone or something somewhere *out there* knows of our existence and our pain and will personally protect and lead us out of our difficulties?

Belief in such a God is wishful thinking, an emotional crutch that inhibits us from becoming accountable and taking charge of our own lives. For just such reasons Marx accused our Judeo-Christian heritage of being the "opium of the people" and Freud dismissed it as a regression into infantile dependency, a delusionary projection of childhood experiences with our parents onto the screen of the universe.

Furthermore, who can take seriously the moral

and ethical claims of a supposedly loving God who, if the Bible is read literally, has the power to alter human nature and/or guide the course of human events so as to avoid human suffering but declines to do so? An all-powerful God who allows the righteous and innocent to suffer is morally repugnant and should be rejected! [5]

And many of us in contemporary Western society have done just that!

Yet my inability to read the Bible literally does not close the book for me. I cannot just put it back on the shelf. In spite of the intellectual unease I suffer when attending church, I find that when I

---

[5] In his book *When Bad Things Happen to Good People*, Rabbi Harold S. Kushner, whose son was born with a rare degenerative disease that led to his early death at age 14, states that, for just such reasons as are set forth above, he was forced to choose between belief in (a) a God who was all-powerful but who either purposely subjected him and his family to suffer pain and injustice or callously failed to intervene to prevent the same, and (b) a God who was not all-powerful and therefore incapable of such intervention. He expressly chose the latter to preserve his further belief in a benevolent God, a God who is fair and just and desirous of assisting us in coping with our tragedies. But to believe in a God who is not all-powerful runs counter to the God generally depicted in the Bible. (Remember the Apostles' Creed description of Him as "the Father Almighty, maker of heaven and earth and of all things visible and invisible.") It also puts our concept of God on a slippery slope. Why should we worship and fall down before a God who is less than all-powerful? If He is not all-powerful, just how powerful is He? Can we depend upon a God of limited powers to answer our prayers? Can He really help us at all?

leave its sanctuary I generally feel more at peace than when I entered. There is something soothing about being enveloped and bathed in the words, music and rituals of Christianity. My tensions quietly slip away. The head rebels, but the heart responds. The Bible's words have an emotional hold on me, and I am compulsively, almost against my will, drawn to them. And it is not just me. For over 2,000 years millions and millions of people have come together weekly to sup and refresh themselves at Christianity's sumptuous banquet table of comforting words, glorious music and shared celebrations and rituals.

But it is the comforting words that most attract me. Why am I so drawn to the words of the Bible? What is it about its images, stories and preachings that resonate in my heart? If reading it literally, as fact, is unacceptable to my conscious, rational faculties, can it nevertheless be salvaged for me by reading it metaphorically?

Returning to Genesis and attempting to plumb its metaphorical meaning, I see that its main narrative thread is God's creation of Adam and Eve, their eating of the apple from the tree of knowledge of good and evil, their becoming self-conscious and their being expelled from Eden, condemned to mortality and having to till the earth for a living. It is a story of birth, separation and exile from a place of abundance, peace and harmony into a place of conflict, dualism and toil. We have all experienced the latter *place* and readily recognize it as a metaphoric description of our conscious, everyday lives on earth.

But the garden from which Adam and Eve were expelled is a mythical, magical, dream-like place. No one has ever visited it or seen its creator and keeper and reported back to us. We have only seen Eden and God as word-generated images and ideas, as emotionally-toned abstractions in our heads. And aha! Doesn't this give us a clue as to the *place* where these images and ideas originated? Aren't these mental pictures and abstractions manifestations of some autonomous energies that exist, so far as we can tell, *only* in our heads and hearts?

The psychologists tell us that whenever an idea, an image or a story stirs up our emotions, grabs our interest, keeps popping into our conscious minds, we must pay close attention. We are probably in the grip of some resonating energy residing in the depths of the unconscious. We are attracted to an idea, an image or a story for a reason, that is, because it satisfies, allows us to express or resonates with some heart-felt, deep-seated fear, need or desire.

If such is the case, Eden then becomes, at least for me, not a place but a vision, a state of mind where conflicting opposites come together to make up a peaceful, communal whole. It is the state of bliss envisioned by Isaiah, where "the wolf also shall dwell with the lamb." It is that which encircles, surrounds and sustains. It is our alpha, our imagined beginning: the protective womb from which we sprang, home and the bosom of our families. And it is our omega, our wished-for end: the promised land, heaven and the paradise to which we would like to return. It is Grandma Moses and her pastoral scenes of abundance and contentment. It is a lighted city on a hill awaiting the weary wayfarer. It is a repository of hope, renewal and refuge.

The common thread of all these emotionally-toned, word-generated images of paradise is that they are projections of a bone-deep, aching yearning for the peace and serenity that flows from being a valued, protected participant in the on-going family of all living things, from being re-united with the place, the matrix from which we sprang and thereby being made whole.

Thus, our psyches have been programmed with what is at once both a yearning for and a vision of paradise, a vision of coming together as a communal whole to live in eternal peace and harmony. A word description (text in a book) or visual representation (a painting) of such vision may take many forms. The details may vary. But when such yearning meets with such a description or representation, they are drawn to one another like magnets and a powerful reverberating resonance is set up in our psyches !

In addition and as the famed psychologist, Eric Fromm, has observed, Adam and Eve's acquisition of self-consciousness is also a metaphoric depiction of mankind's emergence from the primeval evolutionary swamps and our becoming aware of ourselves as entities who exist separate and apart from all other things in nature. We are no longer completely primitive creatures who are only dimly aware of ourselves and must live out our lives as instinctively driven, thoughtless robots.

We have risen above brute nature by acquiring a consciousness of self, the capacity to think for ourselves and exercise some degree of free choice. But we have not risen so far above nature as to have acquired, like the gods, the gift of immortality. The human capacity for reason, memory and imagination enables us to envision paradise, contemplate infinity, grasp the idea of immortality and recognize our uniqueness among all the creatures in nature. But these same abilities force us to realize, with horror, that unlike the gods, our bodies will eventually forsake us. They will slough away and we will die. Just as Adam and Eve were condemned to a limited life span and prevented from partaking of the tree of eternal life, so will we all finally return to nature, to ashes and dust. All our posturing and ambitious striving are, in the end, futile.

When I read the creation story of Genesis metaphorically, then Adam and Eve become us, you and me, and their expulsion from Eden becomes a dramatization of the situation into which all of us are born and how we have come to feel, as Becker put it, set apart, powerless and fearful of our mortality and eventual death.

Genesis also introduces us to the idea of *God*. If the Bible is to be read metaphorically rather than literally, what principles, ideas or psychic energies are captured by the word image of God? When the word strikes our eye, what does it conjure up in our psyches? What do we really mean when we speak of God?

In the creation story God stands for that in the universe which is eternal. He is portrayed as a preexisting, uncaused cause sprung from the void. He is the guardian of the tree of eternal life whose fruit Adam and Eve must be prevented from eating lest they too attain immortality.

God is further depicted as having certain masculine attributes. In Genesis, as well as other parts of the Old Testament, He is shown to be a stormy, authoritarian, law-giving father figure who holds humans to a strict code of conduct. Much is made of His power over us and our duty to submit to His will. It is God who passes judgment on Adam and Eve and condemns them to the harshness of a life of toil and conflict and a limited life span. Such natural calamities as flood, drought and disease are viewed by the writers of the Old Testament as divine punishments meted out on account of wayward human conduct. As Job discovered, God wields such overwhelming power over us that we are to stand in awe and fear of him, as a child before his father.

But the Bible also depicts God as having a number of feminine attributes. He is portrayed as giving birth to the universe and being the source of all life on this planet. He is Mother Nature, the regenerative life force. These creative energies are expressed in cyclic rhythms. When we look to the heavens we are astonished by the orderly, recurring movements of the heavenly bodies. Seasons follow upon seasons. The tides come and go. All living things are born, grow and then die. He is the inexhaustible spring whose clear waters spill out onto the dry land year after year and turn it once again into a green sea of abundance. He is the giver of all we truly need, the air we breathe, the water we drink and the plants and animals that feed, clothe and shelter us. We are dependent on His gifts.

Casting Out Fear

When I add up these metaphoric attributes of God and take into account the Bible's other stories about Him, the Bible becomes, at least for me, an allegory for the idea that there is a link, a connection between mankind and the creative energies and cyclic rhythms of the cosmos. Our very existence, the existence of anything at all, is an inexplicable, gratuitous act of largess extended to us from the beyond that we have done nothing to earn or deserve. Our existence is an act of providential grace, the granting of which we tend to forget. Such forgetfulness causes us to lose sight of the fact that the universe is the matrix from which we have sprung. Our failure to remember such fact further results in our turning our back on the glorious wonder that is the natural world and self-centeredly focusing on ourselves. Such self-conscious, egotistic focus creates a gap between ourselves and the natural world which in turn generates the ache in our heart that is the yearning to be connected to the cyclic, generative processes of the universe and thereby made whole.

The gift of this mythical metaphorical God that most renders the universe worthy of our awe and wonderment is the gift of life: the ability of all living things to replicate themselves in a continuous cycle of miraculous birth, inevitable death and new life once again. This cycle links all living things in a never-ending chain stretching from the simple life forms of the primordial past to our unknown descendants in generations to come. It is our miraculous ability to replicate ourselves that enables us to envision our lives as serving a transcendent purpose, as becoming aligned with the rhythms and energies of the universe and having a prescribed part to play in the larger ongoing drama of the evolution of all living things. All these images affirm our connectedness to one another and the processes of the universe.

It must be noted, however, that the mythical God who emerges from a metaphorical reading of the Bible takes a somewhat indifferent, not always benign attitude towards mankind. He provides the conditions necessary for our existence but doesn't otherwise intervene for our benefit in the historical course of human events. This God does not necessarily know of our individual existence or personally love us and watch over us as a shepherd watches over his flock. This God's promise is only that life, in some form, will go on. He does not promise that humans have been *chosen* to be the paramount life form. He does not assure us of the survival of Homo sapiens. Nor does He promise that, as individuals, we will necessarily find justice in this life or be rewarded for conducting our lives righteously. He promises us only that the conditions for our survival as a species are in place, that the essentials necessary for humans to survive on this earth (if we will but conserve and protect it) are available to us.

I long ago abandoned any literal belief in the creation story of Genesis and the existence of a God as described in the Bible: the existence of a supernatural, all-powerful energy/being, an ethereal someone or something who knows of our existence, watches over us and loves us. Having abandoned such belief, it would have been easy to dismiss all of Christianity's teachings. But the Bible's emotional hold on me was such that I could not summarily let it go. So I reread the jumble of historical fact, myth, fantasy and poetry that makes up the Bible as being mostly metaphor and allegory to see what underlying, secondary message I might discover.

As a result of this metaphorical unscrambling of the Bible, my passage through the labyrinth of my middle years was tortuously slow, and I didn't emerge until well into my 50s. But emerge I did, and the somewhat surprising effect of reaching a metaphorical understanding of the Bible has been to make it comfortable for me to participate in a variety of church services, not just Episcopal services, but the services of many other denominations as well. I no longer become offended or frustrated by whatever literal interpretation or spin a minister may put on various Biblical passages.

The Bible As Metaphor

Coming to a metaphorical understanding has enabled me to step through the door of organized religion and enter its sanctuary without violating my own sense of integrity or feeling hypocritical. And maintaining contact with organized religion, however intermittent, has, I believe, deepened my understanding of the experience and emotional attraction of Christianity. It has also enlarged my capacity for developing a more religious outlook on life.

Chapter 6
CASTING OUT FEAR

Among all my patients in the second half of life that is to say, over thirty-five--there has not been one whose problem in the last resort was not that of finding a religious outlook on life... This of course has nothing whatever to do with a particular creed or membership of a church.

Carl. G. Jung in *Modern Man in Search of a Soul*

I don't know Who--or what--put the question, I don't know when it was put. I don't even remember answering. But at some moment I did answer Yes to Someone--or Something--and from that hour I was certain that existence is meaningful and that, therefore, my life, in self-surrender, had a goal... Led by the Ariadne's thread of my answer through the labyrinth of Life, I came to a time and place where I realized that the only elevation possible to man lies in the depths of humiliation.

Dag Hammarskjold in *Markings*

Casting Out Fear

If Becker's synthesis of modern social/psychoanalytical science is correct, I would expect his findings to be corroborated by those in our society whose sensitivities are most attuned to plumbing mankind's deepest motivations, namely, our literary writers and poets. Therefore, such findings should be reflected in our greatest literary works. In the West the single most widely read and influential literary work has been the Bible. I believe that when read metaphorically and as a masterwork of psychological insights, the Bible indeed confirms what Becker and others have been telling us, even though the Bible's message is conveyed in language quite different from that used by the psychologists. In my view the Bible is not just a series of stories telling us about the interplay between God and His chosen people, the Israelites, and the commandments mankind must obey and follow in order to earn God's protection and beneficence. Instead, it is principally about transforming our thinking and attitudes to the end that we may become different persons. It lays down a thread for finding our way out of the maze of the midlife crisis by calling for the shedding of our fictional, esteem-seeking, socially-conditioned selves and allowing the authentic person who resides *in here*, in the shadow of our hearts and minds, to step forth into the sunlight.

When Jesus was asked when the kingdom of God might arrive, he admonished the questioner not to look here or there, "For behold, the Kingdom of God is within you."[6] He also said, "Except a man be born again, he cannot see the Kingdom of God."[7] The kingdom of God is not a place located somewhere out there in the natural world. Rather it is a state of being to be found only *in here*, in the invisible reaches of our hearts and minds. It is a state attainable only by transforming our thinking and attitudes and thereby becoming reborn as a new person. As Saint Paul said, "Be not fashioned according to the world but be ye transformed by the renewing of your mind."[8]

As I read it, the Bible calls upon us to exchange the fear-based, I-focused, achievement-oriented, esteem-seeking lifestyle for what Jung referred to in the prefatory quote to this chapter as a "religious outlook." In spite of our daily challenges, frustrations and disappointments and the repressed dread generated by our existential situation, the Bible insists that we are blessed expressions and products of the creative energies of the universe. It proclaims that our lives can move forward only if we adopt an attitude of thankful optimism and joyful trust in a providence that will supply us with our essential needs and desires. It holds that we are participants in one immense body of life, that we need one another and such

---

[6] Luke 17:21
[7] John 3:3.
[8] Romans 12:2.

community and fellowship is attainable only by demonstrating a loving, compassionate concern for others. In a nutshell, the Bible tells us that the peace and contentment of paradise are to be found only by shifting the focus of our lives from ourselves to serving and loving others.

When read metaphorically, the Bible's injunctions to "have no other gods before me," to "make no graven images" nor to "bow down to them or serve them" become warnings against being misled in our search for the heavenly kingdom. We must not succumb to chasing after the false idols of fame, fortune and power in the external world. When we fail to obey the *imagio dei,* the image of God that resides within us, when we fail to enlarge upon our capacity for humility, thankfulness, compassion, empathy and love, we may expect to be punished by suffering the loneliness, emptiness and meaninglessness that so often accompanies the narcissistic, esteem-seeking life.

Jesus' announcement in the sermon on the mount that the *meek* and the *poor in spirit* shall attain paradise and inherit the earth is counterintuitive. Since when have the meek become masters? The meaning of such announcement becomes clear only when the Bible is read metaphorically. The metaphorical message is that only the humble, those who do good without any idea of reward or acclaim, those who do not set themselves "above" others will find inner peace.

Those who chase after the delights of status and power are like the Pharisees who "love the best seats in the synagogue and to be greeted and bowed to in the marketplace"[9] and who "love the praise of men more than the praise of God."[10] Jesus constantly rebuked the Pharisees for their vain, self-righteous ways. He also rebuked those who strove after wealth, for "it is easier for a camel to go through the eye of a needle than for a rich man to enter into the kingdom of God." [11]

Much of the literal verbiage of the Bible commands us to fall down before God, to obey Him, to worship Him and honor and glorify His name, as if we are being required to bow down before and yield up our independence to some supernatural, authoritarian ruler residing somewhere *out there*. But reading the Bible metaphorically results in these commands becoming an exhortation that we curb our egocentrism and compulsive striving for the attention and praise of others. Doing so allows an invisible, more authentic, humble, thankful and loving inner self to step forth and become the dominant personality running our lives. In fact, as previously cited, Jesus was quite explicit about this: "For whosoever would save his

---

[9] Luke 11:43.
[10] John 12:43.
[11] Mark 10:25.

life shall lose it and whosoever shall lose his life for my sake shall find it."[12]

Many biblical stories discuss something of value that has been lost and then found after the owner acquires a new understanding, such as the parable of the lost piece of silver[13] or the prodigal son.[14] These are stories about losing our authentic selves, about losing our way by pursuing the esteem-seeking lifestyle only to later find, through repentance and acquiring a greater understanding, the treasure of the divine within. They are stories about rejoicing over one's inner transformation. Take for example the parable of the lost sheep. One out of a hundred is lost in the wilderness. The shepherd finds it and returns, calling on his neighbors to rejoice, saying:

> There will be more joy in heaven over one wicked person who repents, than over ninety-nine righteous persons who have no need of repentance.[15]

It is as if the lost sheep was a person who, in midlife, leaves the company of the upwardly mobile and the socially correct to wander alone in the wilderness of his confused private thoughts,

---

[12] Matthew 16:24-25.
[13] Luke 15:8-10.
[14] Luke 15:11-32.
[15] Luke 15:7.

but who eventually arrives at a new understanding of himself. Thus, a person who has been caught up in the daily heroics of chasing after wealth, power and the esteem of others, but who comes to realize that it is a dead end and repents of continuing such pursuit is in a position to find the treasure of a more authentic, humble and loving self. We should rejoice in such transformation!

But just how do we go about transforming ourselves and unlocking the irons of the repressed existential fears that hold us a prisoner to their compensating desires for success, fame and power? What alchemist's trick do we perform on ourselves to turn dross into gold?

In the quote prefacing this chapter, Jung declares that the adoption of a "religious outlook" is the key to such transformation. What did he mean by such phrase[16] and what must we do to achieve such an outlook?

To reiterate a bit of Chapter 2, as Jung has taught us, the first step to inner transformation must be to enlarge the "I" focus of our ego by consciously integrating into it as many of our unconscious fears, desires and attitudes, particularly our repressed contrasexual impulses, as we can

---

[16] Jung did not define the phrase and what follows is my view of what the elements of a religious outlook would be.

so that we come to a broader understanding of our motivations and why we behave as we do. Our unconscious, hidden attitudes, values and worldviews are shaped largely by our personal, family and cultural histories. We swim in the sea of such attitudes, values and views almost without knowing they are there. And we have virtually no control over the histories that spawned us. We are born into one historical period or another, under one cultural umbrella or another and to one skin color or another. Our families are fundamentalist churchgoers or atheists, entrepreneurs or manual laborers, caring or abusive. We have no choice in the matter.

But we tend to hold the opposite view about what goes on in our heads. We believe we are in charge of our *thinking*, when in fact we are not. As the psychologists have been trying to get across to us, our inner lives are mostly a "mess." We have lost the power to take charge of our lives because we have been, in Becker's word," reinstinctivised," that is, programmed to chase after wealth, fame, power and other proof of our success and superiority in order to earn the esteem of our families and peers. Thus, our behavior has been manipulated by a variety of shadowy fears, compulsive appetites and distorting attitudes and biases operating mostly beyond our consciousness. Essential to inner transformation is an expanded *conscious* awareness of the energies that move about in the recesses of our psyches.

We must come to recognize that our behavior and the emotionally toned *thinking* that informs and drives it is mostly reactive and impulsive, arising from unique patterns of unconscious attitudes, values and worldviews.

It may be difficult and somewhat deflating to admit to ourselves that our ideas and thinking about what we are supposed to do with our lives for the most part has not been shaped and molded by us. Rather, such thinking has been mostly a product of the myths, legends and distorted histories of our culture; our family histories and personal childhood experiences and the compensating desires generated by our repressed existential fears. But coming to such awareness presents us with an extraordinary opportunity, the opportunity, perhaps for the first time, to decline to be blindly, reflexively driven by our reactive impulses, ingrained prejudices and unacknowledged proclivities and cease behaving as cultural conformists and ideological robots.

By eating of the tree of self-knowledge, we may take back what our emergence from the primeval swamps and loss of instinctual drives initially gave us: the gift of choice! We can persist in leading an egocentric, esteem-seeking life, keep on living the lie that we are nothing but our public personas and continue drawing our identity from the racial, ethnic, religious or other group to which we belong. Or we can review the claims and expectations of our families, peers and cultures, break with conformity and our ideological programming and strike out to find our idiosyncratic, authentic, individuated self, the self derived from *choices consciously made* rather than choices driven by unconscious attitudes, values and world views.

Converting such self-knowledge into new behavioral patterns requires, however, that we become truly honest about and responsible for the choices we make. When my esteem is attacked or my status threatened by the acts or words of another, I have a choice. I can respond with knee-jerk compulsivity by becoming angry or resentful and, if I am in a position of authority over the other person, asserting such authority by meting out some punishment or getting in the last word. I can pump myself up with my own importance, righteousness and cleverness. I can rationalize, justify or blame others to deflect my inquisitor's accusations or criticism. Or I can react more reflectively, in a calmer, more caring, kinder way designed to keep open the possibility of maintaining a harmonious, long-term relationship with the other person.

Casting Out Fear

Our relationships with parents, spouses and children are often marked by ongoing, repetitive battles over the same issues. Each party knows by heart the accusatory magic words that will revive all the old hurts and resentments. Both sides are obviously locked into reactive, compulsive behavior. To break up this destructive dance at least one of the dancers must admit and assume responsibility for their contribution to the impasse. It requires total honesty as to such person's motivations in keeping the dance going (most probably the need to be in control, be right and have the last word). Breaking up such dance further requires making a choice about how to *react to* whatever *the other person* has said or done that keeps the struggle going. If we do not assume responsibility for our choices, then we inevitably fall into blaming the other person for the strained, contentious relationship. We become victims.

I may not be able to prevent the toxic emotions---anger, resentment, envy---caused by negative personal experiences, especially childhood experiences, from welling up within me when I recall such experiences or run into the person who was responsible for such an experience. But so long as I allow anger and resentment to hold me hostage, I remain focused on myself, the pain and humiliation I have suffered and the level of care and respect I was entitled to but denied. Greed and jealousy cause me to focus on what is missing in my life, what I do not have. I fear being without even though I often do not know what I want. I become compulsively obsessed by whatever (work, things, alcohol, drugs, etc.) or whoever I grab onto to fill the apparent void in my life. I must exercise some discipline over my reactions to negative experiences and avoid being hypnotized by the past, especially the wrongs inflicted on me by others. I must learn to control how long I hang on to any toxic emotions. Better yet, I should learn to just let them go!

It is also unlikely I will ever be able to call up and directly confront my primal fears of cosmic insignificance, powerlessness and death. However, to the extent such fears' compensating desires (to be in control, acquire more wealth, possess more power and be more successful than my peers) are conscious I can exercise some control over them by simply tempering them, reining them in. I can learn to back off and question how important it is for me in any given circumstance to be in charge and the center of attention. Is winning the argument more important than just clarifying the issue and thereby preserving the relationship? What is the worst that could happen to my esteem if I don't assert myself, if I become a listener rather than a talker? If I do so, would it build the other person's self-confidence and encourage him to take more initiative in the future? What if I let someone else become the center of attention? What would happen if I didn't invoke the authority of my position or lay on a guilt trip? If I let someone else solve the problem or choose the next step even though I think I might solve the problem faster or make a better choice? Would the other person appreciate being given the opportunity to try his own wings? What if I let someone else have his way, even if I believe he is wrong or acting foolishly? Should he be given the opportunity to fail? In many cases, the adverse consequences of my standing aside will be a resounding *nothing* and I will have gained much appreciation and loyalty. I will have made a friend instead of an enemy.

We cannot change others, only ourselves. When we become accountable for our choices, able to choose between alternative reactions to whatever outside events affect us, then and only then do we acquire the ability to shape and change our behavior. We finally take charge of our lives and leave victimhood behind.

Once we become accountable for our choices, our actions and reactions, what would be the next step to the development of a "religious outlook" (an outlook, if we need reminding, that has nothing to do with allegiance to a particular creed or membership in a church)? The word "religion" literally means to re-relate. In my view the relating required is an enlargement of our sense of connectedness to other people and the generative energies of the universe, an amplification of our "spirituality" and sense of being participants in a larger order of life. We need to rediscover the sense of awe and wonder for the natural world we held as children. We need to expand our ability to see the linkages, similarities and patterns that enable us to understand that we are not set apart, isolated and alone, but rather just different facets of one immense, ongoing, miraculous body of life. We must come to know and feel that we are a part of a larger matrix. Our Native Americans have articulated this idea particularly well. In response to a governmental offer to purchase some of his tribe's ancestral lands, Chief Seattle found the concept that the lands were his to sell rather strange, like selling his own mother, saying:

> Every part of the earth is sacred to my people. Our dead never forget this beautiful earth, for it is the mother of the red man. We are part of the earth and it is part of us. The perfumed flowers are our sisters; the deer, the horse, the great eagle, these are our brothers... Whatever befalls the earth befalls the sons of the earth. Man did not weave the web of life; he is merely a strand in it.

We must cease seeing ourselves as self-contained, introspective, self-absorbed individuals who spend our lives busily bouncing off one another, like bumper cars in an amusement park. Instead we need to view ourselves as interlocking pieces of a jigsaw puzzle that, when put together, form a whole in which each of us has an important place and role. When our lives become interwoven with those of others and the world around us, we experience a sense of completeness, of having joined the family of man and all living things. Our lives suddenly become more coherent and meaningful.

Developing a sense that we are valued participants in a larger order requires us to hold onto a dreamlike vision of all living things coming together to live in peace and harmony, a vision of paradise not unlike the Garden of Eden or Isaiah's peaceful animal kingdom. We do not need to go looking for such vision. It is a vision which has been etched into our psyches. We need only to encourage its unfolding, like a bud blossoming into a flower

And central to such unfoldment is embracing the idea, in the words of Dag Hammarskjold as set forth in the quote at the beginning this chapter, that "the only elevation possible to man lies in the depths of humiliation." Humility is the only state of mind that allows us to see ourselves as part of a greater order of life. It does so by dissipating our illusions and forcing us to acknowledge the truth about ourselves: instead of being almighty masters of our fate, we are but bit players in evolution's cosmic drama; instead of being self-sufficient, we are dependent on the universe's bounty for all that sustains us and in spite of the ways we are unique, we are much like others.

Humility teaches us that we cannot enjoy life and attain a state of peaceful contentment living in self-conscious psychic isolation, separate and apart from others. The quality of our lives turns on our relationships We need one another. To be born again requires not just a transformation of our inner lives. It also requires us to be born into the community of other human beings, to become an active, grateful participant in the human family. This vista of our lives as members of such a family, this glimpse of paradise, can only be seen from our knees. We must renounce, as Job finally did, any idea of self-merit, of worthiness, of reward, of status and position, of being entitled to the admiration and respect of others. We must also surrender our desire to have the last word, be in control, to be better and superior to others. Until we do so, we cannot see that, regardless of differences in our gifts or accomplishments, in the color of our skins or ideologies or cultural heritages, we are essentially alike, the intrinsic value of others is no less than our own and all of us must learn to live on this planet together.

Casting Out Fear

Humility puts us on the same level with others, but does not necessarily enable us to reach out to those (especially family members) who we perceive have neglected, belittled, insulted, used or otherwise abused us. So long as we are unable to forgive them, our inner reaction and attitude toward them will be confined to fear-based anger and resentment. We will remain focused on ourselves and condemned to reliving the past, endlessly replaying in our minds the slights and hurts inflicted upon us. Self-righteously seeking revenge and what we rationalize to be justice only leads to continuing conflict and separation, not to compromise, healing differences and peaceful coexistence.

Thus, we must learn how to forgive those who have mistreated and abused us, not so much for their sake but for our sake. We need to muster the courage to open the wound---the sense of helplessness and shame---of being victimized by another as the first step to restoring one's self-esteem. Opening such wound will also serve as a lesson in walking in the shoes of another and turning the other cheek. When friendships and business partnerships go awry, an effort to review the situation from the standpoint of the other person will often force us to recognize that the other person was so preoccupied and self-absorbed in unraveling his own problems or pursuing his own agenda that he was simply oblivious to the impact his words or actions had on you. In instances of physical or sexual abuse, you may discover that the abuser was acting impulsively, out of fears or obsessions over which he had little or no control. Even though you may feel compelled to call the police to protect yourself, you should not necessarily take his mistreatment of you *personally,* as being directed specifically at you. In many instances you just happened to be the one close at hand when something clicked in his head that caused him to lash out and attack you.

Recognizing that the mistreatment you may have received at the hands of another was not directed at you personally will go far in dissipating any fear-driven anger, resentment or hate the abuser's actions may have initially provoked in you. If you do not try to forgive them and hang on to such toxic emotions, you run the risk of remaining emotionally blocked and allowing the bitter acid of such emotions to overwhelm and devour you from within. You risk that you too may become an emotionally numb, uncaring robot. By forgiving, you restore your emotional freedom and your power of choice. And you shift the focus from yourself and put it back where it belongs: on the shoulders of the abuser.

Humility and forgiveness enable us to acknowledge our kinship and reach out for the fellowship of others. Just as the prodigal son returned to his family and the lost sheep was restored to its fold, so must we move from egotistic self-centeredness to active membership in the family of man. The fundamentalist Christian would describe such surrender of our egos as handing over our lives to Jesus. The psychologist would portray it as abandoning the fear-based, achievement-oriented, I-centered, esteem-seeking way of life and redirecting our lives to serving the needs of others. In either case we reach a similar transformational result.[17]

The next step in developing a religious outlook requires us, as with Dag Hammarskjold, to give an emphatic "*Yes*" to *Someon*e or *Something* in our lives in order to make certain that our "existence is meaningful" and our lives have "a goal."

In answering with an emphatic "Yes" to Someone or Something we are called upon to make a leap of faith and imagination: we must hang onto hope; maintain a positive, upbeat, joyful outlook when faced with the unavoidable tribulations of life; we must be proactive in dealing with adversity and suffering (how we cope with an irreversi-

---

[17] At least sometimes. The fundamentalist's narrow reading of the Bible often greatly impedes his inner transformation by entangling him in a web of dos and don'ts or leading him down the path of self-righteous insistence on his own worldview. In such instances he may have difficulty becoming truly humble and reaching out to those who do not share his beliefs.

ble physical disability, being diagnosed with a terminal degenerative disease, etc.); and trust in a provident universe.

To the extent possible, we need to screen out the toxic and the negative and not dwell on the bad things that may happen to us or occur around us. We must show our gratitude and be thankful for the many gifts with which we have been blessed, whatever they may be:

- Good health.

- A loving spouse or friend

- A steady job

- The fragrance of a rose or the warmth of the sun on our back.

At the same time we need to introduce into our lives as many positives as we can, for example:

- Entering into a discussion with a person with whom we have had past disagreements.

- Forgiving instead of seeking revenge.

- Apologizing for a harsh or malicious word said to another.
- Seeking out friends who also have a posi-

tive attitude and avoiding those with a negative attitude.

- Being fair and generous with someone instead of gloating over an opportunity to take advantage of them.

- Looking for the good qualities in a person instead of disliking them out of envy or a pushy unwillingness to share the strings of control.

- Stopping and turning to something more positive when we catch ourselves complaining or becoming critical of others.

In dealing with adversity and suffering, Viktor Frankl has written about his experience of serving as a slave laborer at Auschwitz during World War II.[18] He was forced to sacrifice everything. He was stripped of his family and friends, his belongings, his station in life as a doctor and eventually his own physical well-being. He had only the rags that barely covered his emaciated body. He had no reason to hope that he would be somehow rescued before the whims of his guards, starvation, disease or sheer exhaustion caused his death. He had lost all freedoms and had no con-

---

[18] Man's Search For Meaning, translated by Ilse Lasch, (1959 by Pocket Books, an imprint of Simon & Schuster).

trol over his life save one: the power to choose how he was going to react to his circumstances. Would he allow himself to wallow in humiliation, bitterness and fear? Would he simply give up and surrender to his apparent fate? Or would he summon up the inner resources necessary to choose to endure his suffering with courage, dignity and unselfishness? Only those, Frankl observed, who made the latter choice and were able to hold onto a shred of faith in themselves and the future, only those who answered Yes to Something or Someone, survived the concentration camp.

Developing a hopeful, positive, joyful attitude is a matter of *self*-transcendence, of responding to one's circumstances in a manner other than as might be expected of us. To submissively accept the slings and arrows of life is to live without meaning or purpose. We remain an I-focused victim. To marshal our inner resources and choose to actively and forcefully confront life's inevitable challenges brings a sense of purpose and direction to one's life.

Further, answering Yes to "*Something*" also means dedicating yourself to some task or goal (writing the symphony one keeps hearing in his head, finding a cure for alzheimer's, etc.), to the advancement of some cause (civil rights, etc.) or to the furthering or defending of an ideology (one's religious beliefs etc.) or a set of values (protecting the environment, etc.) about which you are passionate and which *enlightens, inspires or benefits others* without denigrating their world-views or otherwise harming them. When you so dedicate yourself, your life suddenly becomes meaningful and an authentic reflection of who you really are. You cannot find your idiosyncratic, individuated self, the self derived from *choices consciously made* so long as you are focused primarily on self-aggrandizement and your life choices are driven by unconscious attitudes, values and biases.

What is a meaningful task reflective of your unique talents or interests will vary from person to person and may be different at different points in your life. But the common denominators of those who would render their lives more meaningful and authentic by answering Yes to *Something* are the *making a conscious choice as to the task or goal to be undertaken, being committed and willing to make sacrifices to accomplish such task* and *choosing a goal that is other-focused* and not undertaken to simply enhance one's own stature or position.

Alternatively or in addition to saying Yes to *Something* a more meaningful and authentic life may also be achieved by saying Yes to "*Someone.*" As with Dag Hammerskjold, all spiritual traditions hold that the antidote to narcissism, to being programmed by our existential fears to chase after wealth, fame, power and other indicia of our superiority, the cure that will heal the wound of our isolated set-apart-ness and the disastrous effects of our fear-filled, death-denying worldviews and ego-centered, achievement-oriented lifestyles is to enlarge our capacity for kindness, empathy and compassion, that is, love and serve others! As the late Rev. Dale Turner[19] so eloquently put it:

> Love is the active power which enables us to break through the walls that separate us—the doorway through which the human spirit moves from solitude to society and from selfishness to service.

To love and serve another is the ultimate affirmation of the other's existence and value and our life is thereby given a meaningful direction, a purpose! When we in turn are loved by another, we are validated and affirmed by them! We *count*, we *matter*—and our life suddenly has meaning!

And somewhat paradoxically, it is the *giver,* not the recipient, of love who gets the most out of

---

[19] Rev. Turner was the minister of a Congregational Church in Seattle, Washington, for many years. For a number of those years he wrote a weekly column for the Seattle Times, a local newspaper. The foregoing quote appeared in his last column.

serving and loving others. As the giver's self-centeredness diminishes, so he grows in connectedness and his life is enlarged

Love and fear are constantly in conflict and jockeying for position in our hearts and minds. It is difficult for them to occupy the same space. As Saint John observed "There is no fear in love; perfect love casts out fear."[20] Thus, to the degree we are able to moderate and rein in our pursuit of the fear-driven, ego-centered, esteem-seeking life, acquire humility and reach out to others we allow love to rush in and flood our hearts and become the principal motivating energy in our lives.

If we are to close the gap between ourselves and others, then *we* (not some invisible, supernatural energy/being) must be the instrument for making love's power operative in the universe. Our motto must be "love is God" rather than "God is love." We must become enthusiastic, active agents for love's dissemination and choose to respond to all that life throws at us, not with despair, anger and striking back, but with hope, thankfulness, forgiveness and sacrifice for others.

And just to be clear, the love of which I speak—the love which is the emotional wellspring for cleansing our hearts of our existential fears

---

[20] 1 John 4:18

and liberating us from our negative emotions—is not the erotic love of sexual arousal and attraction; such love is centered on one's own satisfaction. Neither is it a compulsive, needy, greedy love limited to just a spouse or a special friend; that kind of love is grounded in fear and the need to be in control or to fill a void. Nor is it a love that extends only to those who dress and think and act just like us, those we call our own—our family, friends or peers in the local community or tribe. It is not just an occasional act of civility or kindness. It is not something we turn on at home or when among friends, but turn off when at work. In truth love is not so much an emotion as an attitude, an attitude that nurturing and serving others is our highest calling. It is a broad commitment to serve and make sacrifices for others, even those we sometimes dislike. It demands that we:

- Provide our employer or customers or clients with the highest level of service, workmanship and expertise of which we are capable.

- Protect, nurture and train the young.

- Assist others in material need.

- Give of our time and extend sympathetic concern to those who are distressed or grieving.

- Give thoughtful advice to those who may be confused or doubt.

- Be a sounding board when others need to vent their frustrations.

- Encourage and be a cheerleader for others when they face a challenge.

A loving attitude also includes a reverent awe and respect for the gift of life and the natural world. For not only is love the means by which we enter the society of our fellow humans, but it is the means by which we become thankful participants in the larger life of the universe.

Chapter 7
EMBRACING COMPASSION

How strange is the lot of us mortals! Each of us is here for a brief sojourn; for what purpose he knows not... But without deeper reflection one knows from daily life that one exists for other people...

Albert Einstein in *Ideas and Opinions*

Be kind. Everyone you meet is carrying a heavy burden.

Rev. Dale Turner[21]

According to Darwin's theory of natural selection, fear—not love—has brought us through the long ordeal of evolution. The theory holds that all animals must kill to live, only the fittest will survive and therefore only the genes of the fittest will be passed on to the next generation. The paranoid, the ever-watchful, the quick-to-strike-back, the strong and the powerful will carry the day and

[21]As previously indicated, the late Rev. Turner was the minister of a Congregational Church in Seattle, Washington, for many years.

assure survival of the species. Darwin's jungle is a predatory, cutthroat world that does not admit to any acts of selfless altruism. Some hardliners of Darwinian theory argue, for example, that stories from the animal world of self-sacrificing behavior to save offspring or other kin from harm are not illustrative of any altruistic impulse, but should be interpreted as demonstrating only an instinctive desire to preserve their genes. Further, displays of altruistic behavior among humans are explained away as undertaken only because of a self-centered expectation of receiving something in return, even if it is just the admiration of others, or dismissed as simply learned behavior imparted by culture's civilizing influences. Certainly the logic of Darwinian theory would suggest that our ability to express empathy, compassion and love for others should have been bred out of us long ago, oozed out of the body of the vanquished in some bloody, reptilian clash occurring on the edge of some ancient, steamy swamp.

But I believe that there is solid evidence establishing that by some miracle we have been genetically hardwired with the ability to love others, and such ability, no matter how dormant or untested in some of us, has inexplicably remained intact to this day.[22] We are born with a built-in

---

[22] In fact I would argue that mankind's success as a species is due not so much to our having an opposable thumb or our enlarged capacity for memory and rational thinking, but rather to

moral compass and sense of justice, an ability to empathize with others and express sympathy and compassion for those in distress. We possess a demonstrable readiness, under some circumstances, to consciously forego our own self-preservation and put our lives on the line to save others. So far as we know only humans have the imagination, cognitive ability and resonating empathy necessary to put themselves in someone else's shoes, to understand that "there but for the shifting currents of chance go I," and the willingness to step in and help or rescue another, even an unrelated stranger, in spite of the risk of great personal harm.

For example, there are those who have given one of their kidneys to a stranger without any recompense, fully knowing that they will die should their remaining kidney fail and they in turn are unable to find a donor. There are many non-Jews who, without any expectation of payment and at the risk of summary execution, generously helped Jews escape the clutches of the Nazis during World War II. The fact that the majority of us routinely accept the responsibilities of marriage and family, undertakings that require a

---

our ability to act in concert, to work together. And our ability to work together is in turn likely due to our ability for seeing others as much like ourselves, our need for their approval and respect, our capacity for empathy and compassion, and sense that we should do unto others as we would have them do to us!

heavy commitment to serving and loving others, suggests that most of us understand (at least emotionally if not consciously or intellectually) the truth of Einstein's observation at the beginning of this chapter that our principal purpose in life is to "exist for other people."

We have an inbred recognition that each of us is a separate facet of one immense body of life. Incredibly, our ability to express empathy and compassion for others extends not just to those of our fellow human beings who are nearest and dearest to us, but even to creatures and other living things outside our own species! The astonishing growth and success of the environmental movement since the early 1960s serves as perhaps the best testament of the degree to which we have become willing to make sacrifices for the benefit of living things beyond the species boundary. The existence and survival of our ability to empathize and demonstrate concern for others within and without our own species is a totally unexpected, wholly unpredictable, marvelous miracle! It may *seem* to some of us as if such power comes from a transpersonal source, from somewhere outside of us, as an act of "God's grace." I would, of course, object to the latter depiction of the origin of such ability. Rather I believe it is simply an unexpected, evolutional gift of nature.

Embracing Compassion

I have spent the better part of my time here on earth looking for the answer to the question: What am I supposed to do with my life? The simple answer—now so clear to me—is to serve and love others! The answer has been there all along, but it has nevertheless (even though I am now in my early 70s) managed to escape my grasp. Why? Why has it been so difficult and taken me so long to discover the truth of this proposition?

The psychologists have never given the topic much attention. But the theologians certainly have been loudly trying to teach us to love one another for centuries, even though they have had only limited success. From childhood on it has been preached to us that we must "do unto others as you would have them do unto you." Yet we are so slow and reluctant to comprehend the heart of this message. It is a message that each person and therefore each generation apparently must hear and learn anew. We have allowed our existential fears of insignificance, powerlessness and death and their compensatory desires for the esteem and admiration of others be the principal energies dictating how we run our lives. And they have led us, not to the certainty of survival but, at least in the past half-century, to the very brink of nuclear self-annihilation!

At least a partial answer to why I have been so slow to grasp this message would be that pursuing the esteem-seeking lifestyle worked for me for many years and there seemed to be little reason to abandon it. As I look back, I realize that I was in my early teens before I became consciously aware of any faint flutterings of empathic concern for others. And by then I was well on my way to becoming addicted to the competitive, achievement-oriented, esteem-seeking lifestyle. The degree of my addiction severely retarded my becoming open to any alternative lifestyles. Like an alcoholic who must hit bottom before admitting to a problem, I had to go through a divorce and a midlife crisis before realizing that the esteem-seeking life was failing me and that there was an alternative. I was so slow in coming to this realization because it required an extensive exploration of the subterranean recesses of my psyche and review of my past life experiences, a process to which I have been somewhat resistant and has been spread out over many years. I suspect my recovery was further slowed by living under the umbrella of the Western Myth and having so many of my friends and other peers in my social niche also engaged in pursuing the esteem-seeking lifestyle.

But perhaps the biggest obstacle to my becoming consistently empathic and supportive of others—and it remains an obstacle to this day—is my controlling/analyzer personality and judgmental attitude! It is my heartfelt desire to be unfailingly kind and sensitive of the burdens being carried by others. But as an analyzer, I live largely in my head. And as an attorney, I have been trained to be suspicious of the motives of others. I automatically look for "worst case" scenarios and hidden motives. I learned early on not to wholly believe the stories that daily came into my office until I had heard the opposing parties' version.

No matter how often I give myself a good tongue lashing, I constantly catch myself making squinty-eyed, judgmental, knee-jerk assessments of other people with scanty or no evidence as to their talents or character. I find myself arriving at opinions about people while stopped at a cross-walk and watching them pass-by in front of me based solely on how they dress, their demeanor, how they carry themselves, etc. I may "admire" a woman's shapely figure from a distance and give no thought to her as a person. I frequently find myself going for the smart-alecky, one-upping quip, trying to get a laugh and impress others instead of trying to get to know them.

Clearly there is a streak in me that sometimes causes me to act like an elitist snob and renders me envious, petty and overly critical in my opinions of others. I suspect the streak is an unwanted but surviving remnant of my need to "keep up with the Jones's," to put others in an unflattering light in order that I appear to be better and more successful. By drawing distinctions between myself and others, I maintain my uniqueness and separate identity. But such judgmental attitude (even when I happen to be right in my opinion about someone else) keeps the focus of my attention on *myself* rather than shifting it to the other person. In effect this attitude pushes them away and puts an obstacle in the path of my walking in their shoes and understanding where they are coming from. By failing to ignore, forgive or otherwise overlook their quirks, shortcomings, vanities and facades, I disable myself from entering into a relationship with them. By not getting myself out of the way, by not taking others as-is and loving them as they really are, I render myself unable to connect with them.

As urged by Albert Einstein in the quote at the beginning of this book, I must keep trying to tear down the illusionary prison walls between myself and others and expanding my ability to express empathy, concern and compassion by:

- Assuming, as did the late Rev Turner, that everyone I meet "carries a heavy burden" (they have lost a loved one, suffer from a health problem, been laid off at work, etc.) and is deserving of my heartfelt concern and help.

- Reacting to willful neglect, rude snubs, insults, unfairness or other forms of mistreatment by others, not by plotting how I am going to get my revenge on them, but rather by seeking to understand what may have driven them to act in such a hurtful manner and forgiving them.

- Questioning the leadership of any political, religious, ethnic or other group to which I belong when they begin to build walls by demonizing other groups.

- Assisting the less fortunate, particularly when such assistance allows me to have personal contact with them and to walk in their shoes for a while.

- Providing counsel to others who may be guilty of serious crimes or other misdeeds or simply guilty of bad life decisions without judging them for their past behavior.

- Withholding judgment and looking for the good qualities in others, while overlooking how they may be different from me and ignoring their shortcomings, alcoholism, obesity, etc.

- Seeing the world through the eyes and from the perspective of another and rooting for someone I initially viewed as a competitor, an enemy or otherwise hostile to me.

Casting Out Fear

I believe I am making some headway in enlarging my ability to serve and love others. But in the spirit of accountability, I have no excuse for how slow and incomplete my progress it has been. Onward!

Chapter 8
AS WE LIVE, SO WE DIE

All is vanity... One generation passeth away and another generation cometh...

Ecclesiastes 1:2,3

Dying is an art, like everything else.

Sylvia Plath in Lady Lazarus

We suddenly appear on earth for reasons unknown to us. We suffer through the usual trials and tribulations of life. And then, without explanation, our bodies cease to function and we disappear, for all we can tell, into the unknown of oblivion. And to be consigned to oblivion is to have no connection to the infinite and eternal processes of the universe and be as nothing in the cosmic scheme of things. In effect, it is as if we had never existed at all!

We try to deal with our inevitable death by denying its reality and repressing the terror generated by the thought of our obliteration. By adopting the "sticking-out" and/or the "immersion in the group" modes of heroic behavior, we further attempt to delude ourselves that our lives have some kind of cosmic importance and that upon our death a trace of our brief existence will continue into eternity. But we eventually learn that such heroic behaviors can carry a steep price in human suffering or are a fraud. They do not grant us the degree of immortality we so desperately seek. Nor do they lead us to paradise, to peace and contentment.

So how are we to accommodate ourselves to the fact that we will inevitably die, leaving only the stench and the worms? Can we ever come to a graceful acceptance of such a degrading and humiliating fate?

Like most of you, I suspect, due to the magic of denial and repression I have no conscious awareness of being terrified by the thought of my own death. Until recently I have held a rather stoical/fatalistic attitude toward my death. It may happen now or later and occur in a thousand different ways. I have little or no control over the timing or the cause. What will be will be. Knowing that death is lying in wait for me somewhere in the shadows of the future, my approach to life in the present has been to move forward with whatever endeavor I wished to undertake, even if it involved some risk of harm, provided the endeavor did not put my very life unreasonably at risk. I see no point in tempting an early, premature death. Mountain climbing, for example, has always seemed to me to be a sport which, no matter how experienced or well-prepared you are, holds an outsized risk of loss of life due to the unpredictable nature of avalanches, the dangers posed by hidden crevasses, etc. But now in my later years, I have come to believe that such a stoical/fatalistic attitude is just another form of head-in-the-sand denial. It does not encourage, but rather brings to a halt, any ruminations on how one might reconcile himself to his own death. It never gets one beyond viewing his death as a consignment to oblivion, an obliteration.

Becker was a professed atheist during most of his adult life, but he came to believe that the only way man could escape from compulsively chasing after some indicia of superiority over others or from submerging themselves in and taking their identity from some racial, ethnic or other group was by plugging into and paying homage to a transcendent higher power. But Becker's higher power was not the God of the Bible as read literally, that is, a benevolent loving God who looks after mankind as a shepard cares for his flock. In one of his last essays, he refers to the Judeo-Christian tradition as "the last comforting religious myth," a myth that has gone "into eclipse," and added:

Casting Out Fear

> One wants to believe that there is a God, even sincerely does. But he cannot take the step to faith, that is, feeling and trusting that God cares about man, can or will do anything to save man. The individuated person is usually left with the problem of the absent God.

He began to use references to God and the divine almost interchangeably with references to the "creative energies of the cosmos." In 1974 at age 49 and close to death due to cancer, in a deathbed interview with Sam Keen he was asked to comment on how he felt now that he was closer to the experience of dying. Becker responded:

> What makes dying easier is to be able to transcend the world into some kind of religious dimension. I would say that the most important thing is to know that beyond the absurdity of one's life...*there is the fact of the tremendous creative energies of the cosmos that are using us for some purposes we don't know. To be used for divine purposes, however we may be misused, is the thing that consoles.* (Emphasis added.)

Becker's equating of God and the divine with the creative energies of the cosmos is strikingly similar to the description of God that emerges from a metaphorical reading of the Bible as described in Chapter 5. Namely, God is a metaphor for the idea that there exists a bond, a connection, an at-one-ness between mankind and the creative energies of the universe.

Just as in dealing with the other challenges of life, the "art of dying," as Sylvia Plath has put it in the quote at the beginning of this chapter, requires finding the right mental approach and attitude. Only through the expression of love---displaying compassion and caring concern and respect for all living things---do we come to see ourselves as participants in the transcendent, larger life of the universe and thereby prepare the way (as did Becker) for a graceful acceptance of our own death.

By becoming active, caring participants in the family of man we become part of a greater community, overcoming our lonely set-apart-ness. By participating and being treated as a valuable, contributing member of such a community, we drink in the power and strength of its numbers and share in its heritage and success, overcoming our cosmic insignificance and powerlessness. And by expanding that community to include all living things, we become participants in the mighty river of life that tumbles out of the immemorial past, courses through the present and carries us all into the infinite generations to come—thereby enabling us to slip on the cloak of immortality, overcoming our fear of death.

Our attitude toward life and how we live in the here and now determines how well we cope with the awful fact of our death. Only as we live a life based on love and concern for others can we die a thankful participant in the creative energies of the universe and part of a transcendent, larger order of life. By living such a life we celebrate the power of love and show others how they too may become active participants in the life-enhancing processes of the universe. Our struggle to keep the flame of love alive ceases with our death, but hopefully those who have been inspired by our example will pick up the torch and fan its flame. Under such circumstances, death becomes an event not to be feared as an obliteration, but a rite of passage: a rejoining with our ancestors, a return to the matrix from which we sprang and a handing off of the torch of love to others.

By leading a life of love, we make each day "count" and, when the last day comes, we continue to "count" in the cosmic scheme of things.

Chapter 9
THE GREEN MYTH

> Gradually I became aware of the old island [Long Island] here that flowered once for Dutch sailors' eyes---a fresh, green breast of the new world. For a transitory enchanted moment man must have held his breath in the presence of...something commensurate to his capacity to wonder.
>
> F. Scott Fitzgerald in The Great Gatsby

With the Biblical myth, at least in Becker's view, in "eclipse," and no longer resonating with many of us here in the early years of the 21st century, the question naturally arises: has any new myth or religion, any new belief system or "ism" emerged from the cultural mists of the West that resonates more loudly with us and is fueled by a similar vision of mankind's connectedness to the creative energies of the universe?

The post-World War II ideological development generating the widest support of all the current cultural trends is the nearly worldwide ecological/environmental movement, a movement not just limited to the preservation of other species endangered by man's encroachment on their territory, but a movement which has broadened into a flood of many interrelated submovements: controlling human birth rates, advocating for animal rights, practicing vegetarianism to avoid killing animals, curbing the consumption of nonrenewable fossil fuels and greater use of renewable energy sources, cleaning up our polluted waters and air, avoiding the further loss of our productive soils through erosion and misuse, recycling waste materials, creating more open spaces by imposing zoning and other restrictions on development, expanding and preserving our wilderness areas, etc.

Our scientists, led by Dr. Rachel Carson, were the first to sound the alarm on the extent to which our industrial-technological achievements, when aided and abetted by the aggressive, highly consumptive lifestyle encouraged by the Western Myth and our pursuit of wealth, fame and power, were seriously, perhaps irreversibly, endangering the natural environment.

The scientists have since been joined by a number of religious thinkers. Among them is the once-silenced Catholic, Matthew Fox, who has been a leader in the revival of a strain in Christian theology he refers to as "creation spirituality." Creation spirituality emphasizes God in His maternal aspect as the life force that pervades the universe and has given birth to all things. It stresses the human need to find a connection with the mystery and power of the cosmos and posits that reverence, respect and compassion for the earth and all of nature, including other people, is the means to finding such connection. It holds that the starting point for religion should not be the patriarchal, judgmental and life-enervating news of mankind's original sin and unworthiness. Rather, it should be the positive, life-affirming news that life is a glorious gift—that we are loved and blessed by nature and nature will sustain us and provide all we really need if we will, in turn, but take care of it.

But with a speed that has been astonishing, the environmental movement has moved far beyond the scientists and religious thinkers. In just a few dozen years, millions of concerned, ordinary people all over the world have rushed to embrace it, each endeavoring in some small way to make a contribution to the perceived crisis. Such outpouring of support suggests that the appeal of the environmental movement does not just revolve around selfishly protecting the well-stocked nest created by the industrial-technological revolution, that its attraction is not derived solely from the hardheaded rationalist's view that our narrow self-interests now require us, however reluctant we may be, to take into account the interests of others, including other species. Rather, such outpouring suggests that these issues have struck a deep emotional chord in us, that once again we are in the grip of powerful resonating energies, of fears and desires lying hidden in the depths of our psyches.

The central inspiration of the environmental movement is the utopian vision---shall we call it the Green Myth?---that we and all other things under the sun are separate but interconnected facets of the eternal, generative life force that permeates all of nature. The Green Myth reverberates with echoes from the past and is a historically conditioned, reincarnated, variation of the many mythical paradises fashioned by human imagination over the centuries—including some of those we touched on earlier, such as Isaiah's peaceful animal kingdom and the Garden of Eden. Just as the Dutch sailors in F. Scott Fitzgerald's quote at the beginning of this chapter held their breath for one "transitory enchanted moment" as they first caught sight of the "fresh, green breast of the new world," the environmentalist's vision of connectedness to the nurturing, generative, life-forces of nature has seized and taken hold of our imaginations. By seeing ourselves as participants in the creative energies of the universe and a larger order of life, we overcome our sense of lonely set-apart-ness, insignificance and mortality.

The Green Myth

What is most compelling about the Green Myth is that it holds out the utopian prospect that perhaps mankind---if we can resolve our other conflicts---has finally fashioned a world view which may eventually bridge all cultures and unite all the people of the earth in one common belief system! Unlike the cultural belief systems represented by militant Islamism, patriotic nationalism, fascism and communism, it does not envision that just one ethnic, religious, racial or other social group or species is superior to all others. It embraces all peoples. And it attempts to connect us with the only thing we know to be infinite and eternal, namely, the ever unfolding life and death processes of the universe.

However, understanding the Green Myth's psychological roots is to also recognize the grave possibility that we may misuse the Myth. In fact the environmental movement has already begun to take on the hallmarks of a religion: a disregard for common sense and verifiable facts, an air of self-righteous and the demonizing of those who are not true believers. While most of us, to one degree or in one way or another, have become environmentally concerned and active, we must be ever so careful not to forfeit the environmental movement to the zealots, to those who would approach environmental matters in a mood of militant, arrogant self-righteousness. We must move forward together rather than act like armed camps.

And we do not all start from the same place. Carefully educating and gently bringing into the fold those who disagree with whatever change we are advocating is a more productive way to proceed. Demonizing those we perceive to be the worst offenders and foot-draggers may cause more dissension than progress. Particularly where economic interests are involved, we must gauge what will be politically supported by more than just a bare majority and make decisions based on hard facts and sound science rather than on scaremongering, what "feels good" and going along with what is politically correct. We cannot ignore the human costs, the anxieties and animosities created by significant changes and dislocations.

Also, advances in the genetic engineering of plants and animals, including humans, opens the possibility that evolution may be taken out of the hands of nature and put into the hands of mankind. It took nature millions of years to produce today's life forms. If evolution is put into human hands, the rate of change is likely to be greatly accelerated. We must be very careful with how we proceed with such technology.

History will be our judge, but the breadth of the environmental movement suggests that it will be a major crucible in which we will find out whether you and I, the latest generation of our species, can in broad cross section transform ourselves by exchanging our fear-motivated, I-focused, esteem-seeking lifestyles for a more other-focused, loving concern for all living things and thereby become valued participants in the ongoing life of the universe entitled to take a tiny sip from the cup of immortality and find a small measure of equanimity in both *life and death*.

LIST OF QUOTATIONS

Chapter 1: Denial and Delusion

Quote from Ernest Becker in THE DENIAL OF DEATH (ISBN 0029021502) at page 4: Reprinted with the permission of The Free Press, a division of Simon & Schuster Adult Publishing Group. Copyright 1973 by The Free Press and renewed 2001 by Marie Becker

Quote from Leo Tolstoy in CONFESSION (ISBN 0393301923) as translated by David Patterson at page 17: Reprinted with the permission of W. W. Norton & Company. Copyright 1983.

Chapter 2: The Invisible Kingdom

Quote from Norman Maclean in A RIVER RUNS THROUGH IT (ISBN 0226500551) at page 2: Reprinted with the permission of the University of Chicago Press. Copyright 1976.

Dreams reported by Edward C. Whitmont in THE SYMBOLIC QUEST (069102454) at pages 43-45: Reprinted with the permission of the Princeton University Press. Copyright 1969 by C.G. Jung Foundation, 1978 by Princeton University Press with paperback addition in 1991 by Princeton University Press.

Chapter 3: The Ego In Irons

Quote from Leo Tolstoy in CONFESSION (ISBN 0393301923) as translated by David Patterson at pages 27-30: Reprinted with the permission of W. W. Norton & Company. Copyright 1983.

Quote from Sinclair Lewis in BABBITT (ISBN0151104212) on last page 401: Reprinted by permission of Harcourt Inc. First copyrighted 1922

Chapter 4: From Here To Eternity

Quote from Ernest Becker in ESCAPE FROM EVIL(ISBN 0029024501) at page 4: Reprinted with the permission of The Free Press, a division of Simon & Schuster Adult Publishing Group. Copyright 1975 by Marie Becker and renewed 2003 by Marie H. Becker.

Quote from Carl G. Jung in MEMORIES, DREAMS AND REFLECTIONS (394702689) as edited by Aniela Jaffe and translated by Richard and Clara Winston at page 325: Reprinted with the permission of Pantheon Books, a division of Random House, Inc. Copyright 1961, 1962 and 1963 and renewed 1989, 1990 and 1991.

Quote from Joseph C. Campbell in MYTHS TO LIVE BY (ISBN 0553209760) at pages 20-21: Reprinted by permission of Viking Penguin, a division of Penguin Group (USA) Inc. Copyright 1972.

Chapter 6: Casting Out Fear

Quote from Carl G. Jung in MODERN MAN IN SEARCH OF A SOUL (ISBN 0151612056) at page 229: Reprinted by permission of of Harcourt Inc. First copyrighted 1933.

Quote from Dag Hammarskjold in MARKINGS (ISBN 03453069960) translated by W.H. Auden and Leif Sjoberg at page 180: Reprinted with the permission of Alfred A. Knopf, a division of Random House, Inc. Copyright 1964 and renewed 1992.

Quote from Rev. Dale Turner in ANOTHER WAY: OPEN-MINDED FAITHFULNESS. Reprinted by permission of High Tide Press. Copyright 2000.

Chapter 7: Embracing Compassion

Quote from Albert Einstein In IDEAS AND OPINIONS (ISBN 0517556014) translated by Sonja Bargmann at page 8: Reprinted by permission of Crown Publishers, a division of Random House Inc. Copyrighted 1954 and renewed in 1982.

Chapter 8: As We Live, So We Die

Quote from Ernest Becker in an interview conducted by Sam Keen published in the April 1974 issue of PSYCHOLOGY TODAY entitled "The Heroics Of Every Day Life: A Conversation With Ernest Becker." Reprinted with the permission of Sam Keen.

Quote from Ernest Becker in an article published in 1974 in issue 10 of HUMANITAS entitled "The Spectrum Of Loneliness."

Chapter 9: The Green Myth

Quote from F. Scott Fitzgerald in THE GREAT GATSBY (ISBN 07432735567) at page 180: Reprinted by permission of Scribners, an imprint of Simon & Schuster inc. Copyrighted 2004.

LaVergne, TN USA
03 January 2009
168769LV00003B/152/P